MEN
of the
ROAD

One Moment in Annihilation's Waste,
One Moment, of the Well of Life to taste—
The Stars are setting and the Caravan
Starts for the Dawn of Nothing—Oh, make haste!
　　　　　　Edward Fitzgerald.

MEN of the ROAD

Charles King

Frederick Muller Ltd

First published in Great Britain 1972 by
Frederick Muller Ltd., 110 Fleet Street, London, E.C.4

Copyright © Charles King 1972

Printed and Bound by
Butler & Tanner Ltd.,
Frome and London
SBN 584 10170 8

Contents

Illustrations

Introduction

The story of the gypsies, or Romanies, as they prefer to be called, makes fascinating reading, interlaced as it is with legend and romance. Many books, some of them containing much romantic nonsense, have been written about these strange people; no less interesting is the actual way of life led by the Romanies in the various countries in which they have chosen to live.

Anyone writing about Romanies is on somewhat shaky ground; in the search for truth and concrete facts, he is often confronted by a barrier of prejudice, ignorance and superstition on the part of both gypsy and non-gypsy. My endeavour is to present the simple facts and truth about the Romany people, and to give, wherever possible, their own version and points of view. In many ways, they are quite different from non-gypsy folk—in their chosen way of life, in their customs, in their desires and in their actual appearance.

Sadly, perhaps, times are changing for the Romanies; their way of life is posing problems for the non-gypsies, and the last of the free people are being forced to conform, to 'toe the line'.

In many countries, Britain included, the Romany traveller

is driven from pillar to post, out from one district into another without rest. The authorities would like him to give up his roaming habits, get himself a regular job and live in a house.

The Romany views this idea with distaste. He and his ancestors have been on the road for over a thousand years; to him, freedom to roam *is* life itself; regimentation and being forced to work in a factory and live in a house spells torture and persecution.

It is true that many travellers have adopted a more settled way of life and live in houses, but very few of them have been true gypsies of pure Romany blood. Which leads us to the all-important question—what is a real gypsy?

⚜1⚜
Who are the Gypsies?

 A GYPSY IS a person belonging to a wandering race which, as far as we know, originated in Northern India. Then why the name 'gypsy'? They were and still are called by this name in Britain, because it was once supposed that they came from Egypt.

At some unknown time, a thousand years or more ago, these people began to migrate, mainly in a westerly direction. We do not know why they decided to leave India, or even if they were already nomadic when they reached there, perhaps from Central Asia. Today, they are to be found in practically every country, with perhaps the exception of some far Eastern ones, such as China and Japan, and no race except perhaps the Jews is so widely scattered over the face of the earth as the Romany.

Upon what grounds do we assume India to be their country of origin? Mainly upon the evidence of the language used by the Romanies; it is believed they came from that country, because a large number of the words are similar to the modern language and dialects of Northern India.

In November 1763, an article appeared in the *Vienna*

Gazette, written by Captain Szekely de Doba, in which he described an interesting discovery. It told of a Protestant preacher named Etienne Vali who was studying at Leyden, and who made friends with some Indian students from the Malabar Coast.

Vali was struck by the fact that their language was similar to that of the Romanies, and he wrote down over a thousand words and their meanings. Later, he met some Hungarian Romanies and tried out many of the words on them. To his great astonishment, they were able to explain the words and their meanings with the greatest of ease. When Vali made this known, many people thought the problem of the origin of the Gypsy language, *Romanes*, was solved—it was an Indian language of Aryan origin connected with Sanskrit.

This was interesting, but it was not cast-iron proof that the Romanies originated in India. Many other people were at this time fascinated by the problem, and the first truly scientific investigation of the Indian origins was undertaken by August Pott in 1844, when he published two volumes, entitled *The Gypsy in Europe and Asia*.

Over the last hundred years, scholars have been trying to establish the exact and original home of the Romanies by reference to their language; to this day, the task has proved impossible with any accuracy, because, in their travels, the Romanies have dredged words from every country through which they have passed.

Some scholars believe that these people were already leading a nomadic life when they *arrived* in India, bringing to that country new words from Central Asia, that they stayed a while, then continued their long slow trek westward. It is probable that the complete answer to the problem will never be known.

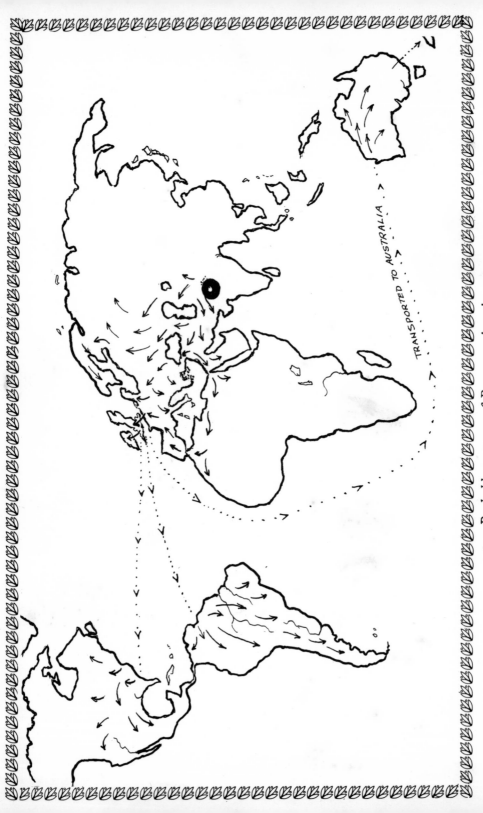

Probable patterns of Romany migration

However, we know much more about the direction of the Romany migration than about its actual date. Scholars who have closely studied the gypsy language claim that they can almost plot the trail they took, since they borrowed forms of the spoken tongues of every people in whose land they lingered. They further maintain that the number of foreign words the gypsies adopted depended a great deal upon the length of time they spent in the country concerned. For instance, Romanes contains a large number of Greek and Persian words (as well as a host of Indian derivations), which seems to point to a protracted stay in those countries.

Scholars would dearly like to know exactly *why* the Romanies left India. Some have suggested that a series of terrible wars or invasions occurred in the areas the gypsies occupied, and they, being nomadic and having nothing to lose by leaving, decided to clear out from the stricken area. But this is mere guess-work; there could be a hundred reasons why the Romanies decided to leave their homeland (if indeed it was their homeland).

In the tenth century A.D., we may assume, hordes of these tawny, black-haired wanderers crossed the frontiers of India in their trek to the West. It must be noted that these people carried with them the customs and occupations of the low-caste Indian tribes from which they may have sprung; they still adhere to these pursuits, in a modified form, up to the present day. The various ways of earning a living forbidden to the higher castes in ancient India included such arts as fortune-telling, entertaining by music, dancing, acrobatics and juggling, metal-working, woodcarving, blacksmithery and horse-dealing, at all of which the Romanies excel. All these jobs are ideally suited to the nomadic life, and in their long journey, the Romanies managed to exist, to pluck a living from the inhabitants of the countries they passed through.

We do not know if the gypsies departed in one huge horde, or in successive waves, but after leaving India's borders, they must have broken up into several separate branches. Therefore it is assumed that after leaving the banks of the Indus, they went into Afghanistan and Persia, some reaching the Caspian Sea south of the Persian Gulf, while others turned towards Armenia, and up to the Caucasus, and on until this branch reached Russia.

Other throngs appeared in due course in Syria, Palestine, Egypt and Morocco. Some of these may have made their way across the north coast of Africa to the Strait of Gibraltar and crossed over into Spain. These migrations took place roughly between the years A.D. 1000 and 1200, and it must be borne in mind that they happened at a very slow pace, the speed of a leisurely stroll.

Sometimes a tribe would decide that it liked the place it found itself in, and would stay; for instance, some families have been living in Spain for hundreds of years, and content themselves with a roaming life within the Spanish border. We know of others who have come all the way from Greece, have wanted to travel about Wales for a bit, then have gone across the Atlantic to America.

By the middle of the fourteenth century, Romanies were recorded as living in what is now Czechoslovakia. Around about this time, too, they appeared on the Island of Crete, and in Corfu, in Serbia, and a little later in the Peloponnese. In 1414 they were noted in Switzerland; Transylvania and Moldavia saw them in 1417, while in the following year they entered Saxony.

Onwards on their roughly west-bound trail, they entered

France, Denmark and Italy, they went down into Spain from France; in A.D. 1500, another wave entered Russia, while the first certain reference to them in Britain dates from 1505 (an entry in the accounts of the Lord High Treasurer for Scotland); there is little doubt that many gypsies had crossed over the Channel into Britain well before that date.

The people who we know as 'gypsies' call themselves 'Roms'. In other parts of the world, the word gypsy has the following equivalents: Zigeuner (Germany), Bohemian (France), Tigane (Romania), Cigány (Hungary), Zingari (Italy), Cigonas (Lithuania), Heiden (Netherlands), Tartars (Denmark and Sweden), Tchinghanie (Turkey), Zincali or Gitanos (Spain), Luri (Baluchistan), Karaki (Persia), Kauli (Afghanistan), and Atsincanoi among the Greeks. These are just a few of the names given by non-gypsies to the gypsies.

On the other side of the coin, the name given by gypsies to non-gypsies is far from flattering; just as the Jews have the word *goï* to describe the Christian, so the gypsies have *gaujo*, which means 'peasant' or even worse—'clodhopper'.

Now, just for a moment, let us consider how we can tell a gypsy of pure Romany blood from a *posh-rat* or a *didakai?* First, a posh-rat is a person born of a marriage between a full-blooded gypsy and a gaujo Posh-rat is Romanes for 'half-blood'.

When a half-blood marries a gaujo, the offspring are called didakais, and are of less than half Romany blood. When these things happen, true gypsies regard it as a very bad example of law-breaking. Gypsy law, which we will discuss later, states that a marriage between gypsy and gaujo automatically brings the punishment of exclusion and banishment from the tribe.

15

And now, how to recognise a Romany, to distinguish him from an ordinary dark person not of Romany blood? Perhaps the most striking thing about real gypsies is their eyes. Their complexions are usually swarthy, ranging in colour from a pale olive to a deep tan—this shows up their white teeth to good advantage. Their hair is black and straight; their noses are usually well-proportioned and of a good shape, as also are the size and shape of their lips. One seldom sees a Romany with thin, mean-looking lips.

On the whole, the average Romany is quite a handsome man, but it is still the eyes that provide the surest guide to his race. There is something about them which is impossible to describe. They are usually very dark and have a piercing quality; they have in them something of the intent look of an animal, and many non-gypsy people are affected by it. There is an uncanny kind of glint or sparkle not seen in gaujos' eyes.

These qualities appear less apparent in the eyes of British gypsies, but with foreign types, those living in Hungary or Romania for example, the effect is particularly striking.

While Romany women are usually graceful in their movements, no matter what they are wearing, the menfolk seem to give the impression of being extremely awkward and badly put together. The Romanies do not have a national dress or costume of their own; they neither make clothes nor do they embellish what they buy with embroidery or fancy work. They dress in the fashion of the adopted country. In Britain, a Romany woman will buy clothes off the peg in a chain store, but she will wear the garments in a way all her own; the same article worn by a woman of non-gypsy blood will appear somehow quite different.

Martin Block, the famous writer, has spent many years studying the Romany people, and in his book *Gypsies* he

A Hungarian fortune-teller

maintains that one can also recognise the gypsy by his walk. He says, 'Gypsies take short steps. One very seldom sees a gypsy walking heavily. If one sees two or three walking together and gesticulating at the same time, one has the impression that they are making a supernatural progress in the course of which it is unnecessary for their feet to touch the ground.'

According to Martin Block, Romany people in general are endowed with extremely supple bodies; they are never flat-footed or hunch-backed, always holding themselves erect when walking. Like many other Eastern people, they rest by sitting on their heels instead of using a chair. They eat their meals and have their family conferences in the same way. Chairs are never to be seen in the tents of genuine gypsies. Often, too, they will take their ease in the cross-legged Turkish position.

Romany women and girls can usually be recognised by their walking and standing movements which are graceful and supple; these are also noticeable with Indian and Pakistani women. Romany women seem to ignore the extremes of fashion entirely. One reason for this may be the gypsy law which requires their women to dress and behave modestly.

Up to now, we have been discussing the genuine pure-blooded Romany; of course there are others who are not real gypsies.

Nobody seems to know the exact number of gypsies and other types of wanderer in Great Britain. The booklet *Gypsies and other Travellers* (HMSO) suggests a figure of at least 15,000 for England and Wales (from a report of a study carried out in 1965 and 1966 by a Sociological Research Section of the Ministry of Housing and Local Government).

Charles Duff in his fascinating book *The Mysterious People* states that in Britain there are about 10,000 true Romanies, about 10,000 posh-rats or half-bloods, and perhaps the same number of didakais. In addition, he is of the opinion that there could be anything from 20,000 to 50,000 other so-called gypsies without a single drop of Romany blood between them. A study of gypsies is made difficult for the beginner because they can be so easily confused with tinkers, mumpers, tramps and other kinds of people who have taken to a wandering life.

The latter are mostly British people who have become nomads for one reason or another, perhaps to opt out from the responsibilities of the rate-paying and law-abiding citizen, or even because of the housing shortage.

Often, many of these folk behave badly, are frequently rude and menacing to householders, leave their junk and filth for other people to clean up, get into all sorts of trouble; and when they are caught, they maintain their innocence, putting the blame upon some unlucky Romany family. They may lead what they fondly imagine to be a 'gypsy life', stealing, causing malicious damage, and being filthy in their habits, but they are certainly not gypsies.

As a real old Romany woman said to me once, "Mumpers! They're a dirty lot of hedge-crawlers. We scorn to go near such low people—a chikli (dirty) lot, not gypsies at all!"

When one begins to study and read about the gypsies, one easily becomes lost in a fog of folk-lore and legend, much of which was created by the gypsies themselves. It has been truly said of the Romanies that 'when they speak in your tongue, they lie; when they speak among themselves in Romanes, they tell the truth'.

19

Many fantastic tales were spread by the gypsies in historical times about their direct connections with Biblical events. One such legend tells how the Egyptian Pharaoh and his army were drowned in the Red Sea whilst pursuing the escaping Jews; all perished, with the exception of one youth and a girl, and the gypsies are their descendants!

Many persons have tried to link the origin of the gypsies with Biblical prophecies. One of these, Reinhold Urban, a friend of the Romanies, put forward the theory that the gypsies were a people chosen by God to show His power and mercy, and quoted the text: 'I will scatter the Egyptians among the nations, and will disperse them through the countries.'

The gypsies themselves, after all, had been regarded as Egyptians when they first came to Central Europe.

At the time of their first appearance in Europe, the gypsies claimed to be descended from Cain, or that they were the smiths who had forged the nails of the Cross, or again that they had stolen one of the nails; their favourite tale was that they were undertaking a seven-year journey of repentance for their sins. All these tall stories were eagerly listened to by the highly credulous and religious public of the fifteenth century.

Dressed in fantastic finery, the gypsy chiefs called themselves Dukes of Little Egypt, and travelled in style from town

Gypsy dancer and singer, Budapest

to town, accepting honours, gifts and money from the people.

When the tawny bands reached North-western Europe, their story about being Egyptians was not believed—they were immediately dubbed 'Tartars' by the Germans, because of their black appearance, their filth, and their nomadic way of life. This did not suit the gypsies at all; they liked very much to be known as Egyptians, because they could cash in on the title—they were annoyed at being confused with the terrible Tartar hordes of the thirteenth century.

The history of the gypsies has fascinated thinking people throughout the centuries. There were in the early eighteenth century some who were convinced that the gypsies were some kind of off-shoot from the Jewish race. They reasoned thus: 'Jews live in ghettoes, gypsies in camps; both live a life spent apart from the rest of the population. Also there is the similarity of the fate of both races, being made to wander the earth for all time.' There seems, however, to be no connection between the Jews and the gypsies; the only similarity is that both races are widely scattered throughout the world.

The sudden appearance of the gypsies in the various cities and towns of Europe during the fifteenth century must have made a deep impression on the inhabitants. Never before had such dark mysterious tent-dwelling folk been seen in such numerous bands.

Naturally, the whole town or village would turn out (leaving their houses and goods unguarded) to stare at these strange beings whose chiefs rode arrogantly by in splendid attire, followed by a caravan of miserable starved horses and ponies drawing loaded carts containing the travellers' worldly goods. The gypsy women and children would beg shamelessly, or slyly enter the houses and pick them clean of all movable articles. They would set up their booths just outside the town, and entertain the populace with dancing bears or with the clever tricks of the monkeys they carried.

Men and women citizens would go and have their fortunes told, and would often come away minus their purses or some other valuable object. Gaudily-clad fortune-telling women would cajole their way into people's houses and steal anything upon which they could lay their hands when the mistress's back was turned.

The merchants in their shops filled with valuable articles of gold and silver suffered particularly when the gypsies came to town; when they had picked the place clean, they moved on.

The chroniclers of the time were all agreed that the 'Egyptians' manners and customs left much to be desired—'They eat like starving pigs, they are disgusting in their private habits, they stink and are full of vermin.'

During the early years of the gypsies' appearance in Europe, however, they could virtually do no wrong. Their lying tales were believed, and they were regarded as true penitents on holy pilgrimages. They were awarded official protection, and many a gypsy chief claimed to bear letters from Princes and Emperors guaranteeing their safe conduct. Regarding punishment for wrong-doing, the chiefs themselves were allowed by official decree to dispense justice according to the 'Gypsy Law' among their own people.

In those early days, the gypsies were treated charitably, but they soon proved utterly unworthy of the trust placed in them. Everybody, everywhere, began to suspect the truth of their pious tales of pilgrimage and penitence. Complaints from every quarter rose sharply in ever increasing number and volume. Town after town, country after country declared themselves to be tired of being shamelessly pillaged by these dark invaders.

Some countries banished them; in others, they were declared outlaws. When they failed to depart, they were hunted down, and the most inhuman measures were taken against them. By now, even the Church had become opposed to the gypsies, because the stories of holy pilgrimages were false and blasphemous, and had been concocted only for the sake of deception and fraud.

By their own conduct, the gypsies had managed to turn every man's hand against them. Far from their position improving, as time went on, their existence became more intolerable.

Frederick William I of Prussia signed an order in October 1725 which proclaimed that all gypsies over the age of eighteen would be hanged if found on Prussian soil. Gallows were set up at the frontiers bearing the words, 'For Thieves and Gypsies', in order to discourage any Romany from entering the territory. As the gypsies could not read, the authorities then put up large warning notices near the gallows, bearing drawings of floggings and hangings which would be plainly understood, even by a gypsy.

By the middle of the eighteenth century, it seems that the whole of Europe was busily persecuting the Romanies. They were declared outlaws in Austria in 1701; by 1726, a general order went out that all male gypsies were to be put to death, while women as well as youths and girls under eighteen years old were to have an ear cut off.

Spain had started a policy of persecution as early as 1492; in order to save their lives, the gypsies left the country, some going south into North Africa and others to Northern Europe.

In France, they had made themselves an intolerable

nuisance, and in 1561 the Orléans Parliament made up their minds to have the gypsies exterminated. The orders could not have been carried out, for by 1612 the gypsies had multiplied so much that fresh orders were issued for their massacre. In spite of such barbarities, many managed to escape to the southern part of France, where today the largest number of French gypsies are to be found.

Important towns in Italy ordered their banishment around 1570; the Scandinavian peoples in Denmark, Norway and Sweden did their best to rid their countries of gypsies by inflicting severe penalties against them.

In England, they fared little better; they were forbidden to hold their own 'courts of law', and were to be subject only to English law (not that there was much injustice in that); but worse was to follow in Queen Elizabeth's reign. An Act was passed in Parliament ordering the death penalty for any gypsy who showed himself in England one month after the Act became law.

By this time, large numbers of gypsies were to be found in every country in Europe; each one in turn tried to rid itself of the dark strangers by means of harsh laws, constant persecution, and savage penalties. But for all this, none of them succeeded. In the face of such mass hostility, it is a miracle how the Romanies were not only able to cling to life, but were able to multiply and spread, for according to the experts, there are today some five or six million real gypsies scattered throughout the world.

A happier era dawned for them in the second half of the 18th century, when attempts were made to educate and civilise them and to turn them into settled citizens. Queen Maria Theresa of Hungary and Bohemia took them under her wing in 1761, naming them 'the New Peasants' or

A bear-leader

'Neo-Magyars', because she thought the epithet 'cigány' (gypsy) was an insulting one.

The good Queen's motives were of the highest, but she showed a total lack of understanding about the gypsies and their way of life. For instance, she thought that living in tents should be beneath the dignity of her Neo-Magyars, so she forbade them to live in the open; she tried to stop them using their own language, and ordered them to cease their trading in horses. They were no longer allowed to elect their own chiefs, and worst of all, to get them used to European customs, gypsy men were conscripted into the army, while the gypsy children were compelled to attend schools.

This, one of the first attempts to integrate an alien people, failed dismally, owing to the complete misunderstanding of the gypsies. In the reign of Joseph II, the Queen's successor, forty-five gypsies were sentenced to death for alleged cannibalism. Although too late to obtain a reprieve for the victims, Joseph was able to establish the fact that no proof whatever had been produced.

During his reign, he also tried to suppress the wandering instincts of the Romanies, and to make their children attend schools. A terrible uproar ensued when the soldiers, sent to take the children away from their parents, dragged the youngsters away with ropes.

A much happier result was obtained by a Hapsburg prince, the Archduke Joseph, who succeeded in persuading many of the gypsies in his domain to settle on one of his great estates. He did not try to 'convert' them to civilised ways, and allowed them to live as they pleased. His hope was that they would learn to settle down of their own accord, but after he died, his bands of gypsies broke up and scattered to the four winds.

In 1783, Charles III of Spain made an attempt to settle the Romanies on the pattern tried by Maria Theresa. He even went to the length of calling the gypsies 'Neo-Castilians'; he too forbade them to use their own language, and wished them to give up the nomadic life and work at an honest trade. Many were indeed persuaded to settle down, and some of them adopted new ways of earning a living, such as slaughter-house men, eating-house keepers, and even bullfighting.

It is interesting to note that during the cruel days of banishment in Spain, many Romanies overcame their deep dislike of long sea journeys and left for South America, where they founded families in Brazil, Chile, Argentina and other South American countries.

By now it seemed that the period of cruel persecution was over, and governments were becoming more liberal and humane in their approach to the gypsies. Brave attempts to create settlements were made in several parts of Germany, but they failed, owing to lack of knowledge of gypsy ways and customs on the part of the authorities.

The Poles had greater success, for their efforts were attended by a deeper understanding of the Romanies' needs. The gypsies were able to live unmolested in Poland, and they even *encouraged* their children to attend schools. Lithuania, too, was kind to the nomads, and large numbers were able to live in that country without fear.

Martin Block tells us that the greatest success of all was achieved by the efforts of Catherine II of Russia, who settled the Romanies as serfs on Crown lands; Russia, it seems, has always been moderate in her approach to the gypsies—in the past, there were even several instances of aristocratic Russians marrying gypsy dancers.

In Romania, the gypsies were slaves. The great estates of the Boyars or landowners were growing wild because of man-power shortage, and they greedily seized the chance of com-mandeering this army of free labour to work their fields and vineyards. The gypsy in Romania at this time belonged, body and soul, to the Voivodes, the Boyars and even to the clergy; they had no rights whatever, no wages, and the food given to them was of the poorest and most meagre. The landowners 'employed' gypsies in their households as domestic workers, coachmen, scullions, musicians and so on, and woe betide them if they showed the slightest sign of rebellion—they soon felt the whip around their backs, or the cane of the bastinado on the soles of their feet. In those evil days, it was no crime to kill an escaping gypsy slave, or to submit him and his loved ones to the most frightful ill-treatment.

The Romanian peasants themselves suffered from the

cruelties of the nobility, and it was sometimes to them that the gypsy turned for a crumb of comfort.

A Romanian noble of a very different kind, Alexander Ghică, began a campaign in 1837 to try and get slavery abolished, and a Bill was introduced in the Moldavian Assembly in 1844 with the object of freeing at least the slaves of the priests and clergy. Another Voivode of the same name, Gregory Alexander Ghică, finally won the fight to free the gypsies in 1855, when 200,000 of them were liberated, given Romanian nationality; at the same time, the State declared a general amnesty for any gypsy outlaws who had taken to the forests and mountain caves to escape the inhuman treatment of the nobles.

2
Gypsy Tribes and Occupations

 IT IS VERY rare to hear of a gypsy living alone. He likes the company of his own people, the lively talk and doings of the day, so in the world of the Romany, the basic unit is that of the family. Although they may not see each other for months, families can keep in touch with each other by word being passed on, the use of sign language, the *patrin*, or other methods best known to themselves; sometimes, when something important is afoot, they will use the Telegram Service.

A whole group of families may live and move about together, and these will probably be part of a clan. Many clans go to make a tribe, and these tribes in their turn make up other units which, for want of a better word, could be called 'main stems'.

There are three of these principal 'stems': The Kalderashi, the Gitanos, and the Manushi.

The Kalderashi

These gypsies are of the opinion that they, and they alone, are the only genuine 'true black Romanichals'. They are mainly workers in metal—tinsmiths, coppersmiths, and so on

—and they came from Eastern and South-eastern Europe. It is said that some of the Kalderashi have fair skins; Charles Duff has heard of Kalderashi with fair hair and blue eyes.

This stem is divided into five groups as follows:

The Lovari, called Hungarians, because they stayed a long time in that country.

Boyhas, from Transylvania, whose speciality was the exhibition of animals.

The Luri, who still bear the name of an Indian tribe.

The Churari, makers of brooms and brushes.

Turko-Americans, called thus because they emigrated to America direct from Turkey before returning to Europe.

The Gitanos

This group apparently prefer to stay in a specified area comprising Spain and Portugal, the South of France and North Africa. They are a very dark-complexioned people, and they divide themselves into three groups, Spanish, Catalan and Andalusian.

The Manushi

This group are also called Sinti, perhaps because of an origin in the region of the River Sind, in India. The word 'manush' is derived from the ancient Sanskrit word 'manusha' for 'man'. The Greek gypsies use manush for 'man' and manusha for 'woman'.

The Manushi divide themselves into three sub-groups: the Valsikanes, showmen and circus people (French); the Gaygikanes, (German); and the Piemontesi, (Italian). Nearer at home, of course, we have Romanies who have made their home in England, Wales, Ireland and Scotland. Some of them are said to resemble the Kalderashi and Manushi, although it

32

Bowl-maker using curved adze

is improbable that any British Romany family would know to which group it belongs. In Europe, clans are known to each other by words which call to mind the trades in which each specialises, for example:

Ursării—Bear-leaders, still to be seen in South-eastern Europe.

Chivuţi—Women who make and sell whitewash brushes.

Churării—Makers of brooms.

Caldărarii—Tinkers.

Selling flutes in Romania

Ferării—Iron-smiths (horse-shoes, ironwork for doors and gates).
Costărarii—Workers in copper.
Lingurării—Makers of wooden spoons, wooden articles for farmers.
Potcovării—Blacksmiths.
Spoitoresele—People who whitewash the fronts of houses.
Mesteri-Lacatachi—Iron-smiths and locksmiths.
Lăutarii—Musicians.
Vînzătoarii—Flower sellers (women).
Vrăjitoarele—Fortune-tellers (women).
Ciobatorii—Boot repairers.
Salahorii—Masons and bricklayers.
Rudari—Makers of wooden bowls, plates, axles, etc.
Vatrachi—Gardeners (house-dwellers; *vatra* is a fireplace in Romanian).

There is no doubt that the gypsies are the world's most accomplished beggars. They are real artists in managing to extract small sums from the pockets of soft-hearted gaujos by displays of pity or by flattery. Well, no one is much the worse off for that. In the Northern parts of Europe, the habit of begging has brought unpopularity upon the gypsies. What can be the reason behind the habit, and why is it that they see no shame in it?

For the answer, perhaps we could look back to their supposed Indian origins, and recall that they brought with them the customs and occupations of the low-caste tribes from that country, earning their living by singing, dancing, tinkering, telling fortunes and begging; we can only assume begging is in their blood.

However, there are several occupations in which the gypsies

excel; they are good smiths and workers in all kinds of metals, ferrous or non-ferrous, and in precious metals like gold and silver. They are musicians, and in this profession they can be truly superb, but as performers only, not as composers. They are good at everything to do with horses; various kinds of woodwork and wood-carving; singing and dancing, and the arts of foretelling the future.

The intriguing question must now be asked—why do they always seem to choose these trades, and why are they so good at them? Again, part of the answer leads us to India, where such work was forbidden to upper-caste Indians with their strictly defined occupational and religious taboos. Another and more obvious reason for their partiality for such employment was that each one was very suitable in a life of nomadism.

It is a passing thought, but maybe certain gypsy tribes accompanied the nomadic Mongolian hordes of Batu Khan, where they rendered good service by arrow, sword, spear and shield making and repair. Vast quantities of these weapons were required by Batu's army; the gypsies could be counted upon to care for the horses, ponies, mules and camels, and could make themselves useful by repairing the yurt-carts, making felt to cover the yurts, and the thousand and one jobs needed by an army on the march.

Each branch of the metal men deals with a particular metal; there are articles to be made in iron by the smith who uses hammer, fire and bellows; the plate and sheet iron beater who works without fire; the copper-smiths who use sheets of tin and copper, afterwards fastening the vessels and receptacles with solder and rivets; the tin platers, who plate over other metals, and finally, the craftsmen who make and engrave precious metals into jewellery.

Wooden spoons and pegs, Bucharest

The horse has practically disappeared from our roads as a beast of burden, but the automobile has taken its place with a vengeance. Here the modern Romany, with his skill and aptitude with all kinds of metal, comes into his own, whether it be panel-beating or car-breaking. He is as good with a car as his ancestors were with a horse.

Martin Block has himself seen the gypsy copper-smiths at work in South-eastern Europe. With the most primitive portable anvil, a hammer with a highly polished flat head, and the skill of their hands, they work at a pan or cauldron until the holes disappear and the bottom looks like new again. Some of the pots Block saw were normally only good for scrap, but the gypsy patiently worked at them until they were water-tight and fit for use.

The men who work in iron are equally clever. In their capable hands, the metal seems to know its master, and nails, horse-shoes, ploughshares, locks and bolts, tools such as choppers, hammers and spades are turned out in the primitive hut or shack used by these men who have settled on the out-skirts of the town. The itinerant smith carries his meagre equipment in a leather bag, and can set up for business wherever he is needed. His little stone anvil is sunk halfway into the ground, a bellows of goatskin fans the fire, and his tools consist of a couple of hammers, two pairs of pincers, a file, and a pair of snips.

He sits cross-legged on the ground, works the bellows with his left hand, and holds in his right the pincers which secure the piece of iron to be worked.

Today, cheap factory-made articles have taken away the livings of many gypsy smiths, and they are obliged to use their traditional skills in the fields of industry. In France, for example, they are valued as boiler-makers and repairers;

others have found work in light engineering and in garages repairing and overhauling cars and lorries.

Gypsy slaves were employed in earlier times in Hungary and Romania, on gold-washing in certain rivers, and were called *Aurării* or *Zlatării*. The sand and grit contained quantities of gold particles, and the method used to recover the metal was as follows; Wooden planks with deep grooves in them were thrust into the fast-flowing streams at an acute angle, facing the current. The grooves collected grit and fine sand

A Hungarian gypsy smith poses with his anvil and bellows

Tinsmith on the outskirts of Bucharest

which was emptied on to a flat platform; the gold particles could then be picked up by using a ball of clay.

The nomadic wooden sieve-makers still manage to make a living in South-eastern Europe, and travel about the countryside, sleeping in the open in their tents. They use donkeys to carry their household goods and equipment for their trade, and call at farms and attend the markets in the country towns; the peasant women prefer their products to the mass-produced article, because they are strong, hard-wearing and hand-made throughout.

In the great Obor market in Bucharest, the gypsy women are to be seen displaying their hand-made brushes on long poles which are used for distempering cottage walls. One can buy the brushes, or members of the family will come along and do the white-washing themselves.

Also to be seen, mingling with the busy throng in the hot sunshine, are the Romany women hawking clothes-hangers or the pegs which their men-folk have made. I have bought wooden spoons from other gypsies in Pitesti, a town in the south of Romania, as well as flutes made of wood. These have a particularly sweet tone. The spoons, which are severely practical in design, are made of soft-woods such as willow or lime, and cost the equivalent of fourpence each.

Hungarian women pedlars

Large wooden 'dolly-tubs' for laundering, wicker carpet beaters, and many other kinds of household goods made by the Romanies were on display in the market; noticeable too, were the dark-complexioned fruit sellers with their stands and barrows. They live a settled life in shanty-type dwellings on the outskirts. Another group who make their living entirely from objects of wood are the *Rudari*; they not only carve, but use a primitive form of lathe for turning round articles. Spoons, bowls, bakers' shovels or 'peels', trunks and chests, toys, in fact everything that a farmer or peasant needs, is made by the Rudari.

For colour decoration, the typical gypsy sources are employed—greens from certain leaves; bilberries for a blue, other berries and types of fungus for reds, yellows and browns, while soot serves for black. It is interesting to note here that the Mongols in Central Asia use similar methods for obtaining colours for dyeing cloth.

Basket making is a typical Romany industry and one not likely to be displaced by the machine. Gypsy basket-work is strong and long-lasting, because it is entirely hand-made. Flowers, made from wood shavings and resembling chrysanthemums, are also produced, while mats made from rushes, or rush-work sunblinds, still find a ready market.

Perhaps you have seen the large 'Ali Baba' linen baskets on display in your local shops; some of these come from Romania and are most probably made by gypsy hands. Some years ago, it was possible to find on display in hardware shops in Britain, gypsy-made wicker carpet-beaters in several traditional designs, but whether the Romanies still make them and supply them to the stores, I have no means of knowing.

In the streets and markets of Budapest and Bucharest, the *vînzătoarii* or women flower sellers are a gay feature. Often,

Gypsy shoe-blacks, Bucharest

a pretty gypsy child is to be seen going the rounds of the tables in the restaurants proffering her posies. Usually, her hopeful shy smile is too hard to resist, and she soon leaves, grinning broadly, two or three lei the richer.

The Romany shoe-blacks ply their trade in many Romanian towns and cities. The customer sits on a high seat, a little awning shielding him from the sun, while the expert gets to work with his assortment of tins, bottles and brushes, first however inserting two cardboard shields at either side of the ankle (to protect the customer's socks). Very soon, a brilliant effect is achieved, and the dark face of the Romany looks up with a smile and a flash of white teeth.

We now come to the occupation which the Romany loves the best, that of being with and dealing in horses. It has been said that to work with horses is the noblest of professions and the only one worthy of a gypsy. Many Romanichals assert that a gypsy without a horse is not a true gypsy.

Nevertheless, it is very strange that, in spite of his admiration for this animal, the Romany is a poor horseman.

Their attraction to horses may be inborn like their begging, their smithery, their music and entertainment handed down from their Asiatic days. The Mongols and Tartars of Asia have the same feeling for the horse, but are superb riders; *they* feel awkward and clumsy when they are forced to walk!

It is sometimes hard to believe that the gypsies' love for horses is genuine, because of the cruel methods to which they occasionally resort in faking up broken-down horses for sale. It must, however, be stated at once that horse-trading gypsies really know their job, and many of them are highly skilled in the doctoring of sick horses.

True Romanies have a wide knowledge of herbal cures both for horses and humans—they very rarely call in a doctor. While the gypsy man will treat a horse, it is mostly the woman who is the 'doctor' in the family. She is also a chemist; her remedies and prescriptions are hundreds of years old, and are handed down from her mother and grandmother, and will be handed on to her daughter.

Many are the tricks still used by gypsies everywhere for the purpose of horse-faking, and which still deceive the gaujo population. In order to make a poor old animal look sprightly at a sale, they may, before taking him to the market, violently shake a tin pail containing stones under his nose until he goes almost mad with fear. Then, at the market, when a likely customer is secured, it is enough even to *show* the pail

to him, even from a short distance. At the sight of it, he will prance and cavort like a fiery war-horse.

Gypsies have been known to make a horse appear hopelessly lame, by secretly inserting a piece of copper wire into a little cut made in its hoof. In a short while, the wire will cause the wound to fester; the gypsy will then cajole the owner into selling the lame nag for a low price. If the deal comes off, the artful gypsy is easily able to effect a quick cure.

To disguise a horse's age, its teeth are filled; holes are bored in the teeth with an awl, the holes are filled with birchwood which very soon goes the same colour as the teeth.

To make an animal look frisky and hold its tail out in the style of an Arab stallion, the horse-loving gypsy will insert a piece of ginger into it under the tail. Another example of faking; perhaps a horse has been purchased from a gypsy—it seems to be in pretty good condition, but after a few days, the effect of the drugs and dope which have been administered to it wear off, and the poor old creature stands before its new owner, a shadow of its former self.

It is not, of course, only gypsies who practice these cruelties, and who fake horses for sale. On balance, the gypsy is no more cruel to animals than the gaujo; when it comes to children, the scales are heavily in favour of the gypsy—it is extremely rare to find a case of cruelty to children committed by gypsies.

Gypsy women have been renowned for centuries for their skill in the art of Cheiromancy, telling fortunes by the lines of the hand. The word the British gypsies use for fortune-telling is dukeropen or dukerin'.

Gypsy women have always pretended to possess second sight, and their 'gift' for foretelling the future seems remarkable, even uncanny. However, it is not quite as uncanny as it seems, for the gypsy, besides reading the palm, has a sharp eye for character, and during a palm-reading session, will be quick to notice facial expressions—a loose-lipped mouth, or a face with thin lips and mean-looking eyes.

The hands will often betray the client's occupation; his manner of dress, too, may be of help in her 'forecasts'—with so much material at hand, it is no wonder that the gypsy, a born psychologist, can quickly size him up, and tell him things about himself he never knew before!

Death, love, money, bereavements, travel, health and long life are the things the gaujo client wants to know about concerning himself. Most people have a superstitious streak in them—witness the thousands who eagerly read their horoscopes in the papers every day.

For the gaujo client, be it a pretty young girl, a handsome youth, a tired businessman or a worried housewife, there is mystery in the dark eyes and face of the gypsy with her impressive tones and outlandish dress as she carries out her dukering in a dim little tent. Of course, people are not really deceived—they would *like* to believe, but they enter into the spirit of the game and are prepared to pay a little for the sake of the fun.

Gypsies never practice the art among themselves; it is strictly for the benefit of the dinilo gaujé (foolish gentiles). While their husbands are away working as horse-copers, metal-workers, etc, the gypsy wives go the rounds door to door with their baskets of produce, and can sometimes get the peasant's wife to 'cross her palm with silver'.

Playing cards are sometimes employed in fortunetelling, but this method is mostly used at fairs, where the gypsy can set up a little booth furnished with cloths adorned with mystical signs, and with perhaps a crystal ball.

Abroad, tarot cards are used as aids in fortunetelling. These cards are quite different from British playing cards and have seventy-eight to a set; their shape is more oblong and they have completely different designs on their faces.

Other objects and substances are used universally by gypsies for the purposes of divination, such as mirrors, tea-leaves and coffee grounds, beans, molten lead dropped into water, burnt bones. We are probably more familiar with the tea-leaf method in Great Britain; many have been the journeys, the dark strangers and unexpected letters seen in the bottom of a British tea cup. Here is a British gypsy poem about dukering, in the gypsy language, which appears in the Rev. George Hall's book *The Gypsy's Parson*.

Mandi's chori phuri dai
Jaw'd adre kongri to shun the rashai,
The gauje saw sal'd as yoi besh'd talé.
Yoi dik'd 'dre the lil, but yoi keka del-apré
The rashai rokker'd agen dukerin, pen'd dova sos a laj
But yov keka jin'd mandi duker'd yov's chai
Puker'd yoi'd romer a barvelo Rai.

Here is the translation:

My poor old mother
Went to church to hear the parson
The gentiles all laughed as she sat down
She looked in the book, but she could not read,
The parson talked against fortunetelling, said it was a
   shame,
But he never knew I had told his daughter's fortune—
Told her she'd marry a wealthy squire!

While on the subject of Romany occupations, one often sees a circus turn described as a 'gypsy act'; the persons concerned may give a brilliant performance and may even have a drop of Romany blood, but they are unlikely to be pure-bred gypsies. It could be that they describe themselves so, to give some extra glamour to their act.

The group of gypsies who have taken to circus life whole-heartedly are the *Valsikanes* or French Sinti; these people have learned how to tame lions, tigers and other wild animals since they first had contact with circuses. Every year, Paris and other French towns are entertained by menageries of wild creatures, which have been tamed or made stupid by the usual barbarous methods of pain or hunger.

A similar show is put on by the Bouglione family, who belong to the old tribe of Italian Sinti.

The Ursarii or gypsy bear-leaders can still be seen in parts of South-eastern Europe, though it is believed the trade is dying out; and a very good thing too. Cruelties are inflicted on the young bears in order to train them to dance, although when their training is over, things are not so bad for them. More sophisticated amusements like football matches and the television have sounded the knell for such primitive entertainment.

The *Salahorii* are masons and builders. Some have taken to a settled life and live on the outskirts of various Eastern European towns, while others still prefer a nomadic life, taking their tents and carts, and camping near their building site.

'Sweet Lavender, Lady?'
(*English, 1910*)

⦿3⦿
Music

WE ARE TOLD by the old Persian poet Firdusi (who lived round about the year A.D. 1000) that a Persian King, Bahram Ghur, invited some musicians, called the Luris, to come to his country to cheer up and entertain his subjects who were feeling sad and depressed for lack of amusements.

Firdusi tells us that over 10,000 gypsy minstrels, both men and women, came at the King's request; he generously gave the incomers land, corn to sow, and livestock to rear on the condition that they kept their part of the bargain and amused his subjects.

At the end of one year not one acre had been ploughed, they had eaten the corn and the cattle, and found themselves without means of livelihood. The King was disappointed and very angry, took away their donkeys and musical instruments, and told them to go and sing for their living.

Certain tribes or groups of gypsies have been minstrels for as far back as records exist, and today, in many European and near Eastern countries, their performances are as popular as ever. For more than a hundred years, scholars have tried to reach agreement on the question—'What is Gypsy Music?'

Franz Liszt was of the opinion that the music played in his day by Hungarian gypsy bands was *original* gypsy music; contrary to this view, many folklorists and musicologists maintain that the Magyar peasantry were in possession of their musical folklore centuries before the gypsies entered Hungary, while Béla Bartok said the chief musical talent of the gypsies lay in their ability to *transform* any folkmusic that comes to hand. To call them simply adaptors is hardly just, for they can be brilliant innovators, just as the old Negro masters of jazz could extemporise on a simple dance tune and create a jazz masterpiece.

It is a fortunate thing for us that the two elements, Hungarian music and the gypsy performer, blend together so wonderfully; both have Asiatic origins, and this may be the reason for it. However, no matter what country in which the gypsy has chosen to live—Romania, Russia, Bulgaria—he will take the peasant's simple and unadorned folk-air, give it the gypsy treatment, and play back to him a piece be-jewelled, enriched and embroidered, to the peasant's delight.

Gypsies in general are illiterate and have no system of writing. Musical scores mean nothing to them, and this is the main reason for the absence of written gypsy music. (There are exceptions to this in the Socialist countries; if a gypsy musician has an ambition to join one of the State Folkmusic Ensembles, he has to attend music school.)

The typical gypsy player has no need of written notes. He carries hundreds of tunes in his head; he has a wonderful gift also of being able to hear a new tune just once or twice and then he's got it. Once, in a restaurant in Hungary, I called the primás (leader of the gypsy orchestra) over to my table and asked him to play 'Greensleeves'; he had not heard of it, so I hummed the air through to him just twice. He put his fiddle

Left, gypsy cobza-player; right, Fanica Luca, world-famous player on the panpipes

to his chin, faced the band and played it over to them. All their dark eyes were on him, listening intently.

He began the tune again, then they all joined in—and how they transformed that simple English air! Violins, clarinet and cello blending in a sweetness of sound, while the running chords of the cimbalom wove a pattern of sonorous fire.

To sum up, when one hears 'gypsy' music, one is listening to the transformed and adapted folkmusic of some other race of people.

Have the gypsies a music of their own? Does an independent gypsy folksong treasure exist, and can the Indian origins of their melodies be proved? I would say that no proof what-

53

ever can be offered to the last question, but regarding the first two, to anyone who has heard the gypsies singing in their own language, the answer must be yes. Their own music is quite independent and differs greatly from that of the surrounding people, just as gypsy costume is independent, despite the fact that the Romany woman buys every single piece of her dress in the average gaujo dress shop.

The instruments and tunes they normally play have nothing in common with their genuine folksong. Instead of using instruments, singing is accompanied by tapping of feet, clicking of tongues, and knocking on the table. The sound is said to recall Indian singing accompanied by the drum or tabla, and is a sort of droning noise, not very melodic to Western ears.

In the Hungary of long ago, every great lord had his own gypsy orchestra; Queen Beatrice, wife of Mattyas Corvin (end of the fifteenth century) had gypsy musicians in her service.

Gypsy players led the way in great processions and national celebrations, they led armies into battle, and at the end of the 18th century, they assisted the recruiting sergeants, by playing the 'Verbunkos'. This was a stirring dance featuring violins, clarinets and cimbaloms, which caused the recruits' hearts to beat and eyes to sparkle with martial fervour.

Out of all the instruments, the violin is the chief love of gypsy musicians. It is vital to them, and it has often been said that they cannot live without it. The question arises, what did the gypsies play upon before they encountered the violin?

The violin is not an ancient instrument; during the middle ages people played rebecs and viols—it was not until after 1600 that the Italian master craftsmen perfected the violin as we know it today. There existed 'fiddles' in 1550 with four strings which were tuned in fifths; some years before this, players used a three-stringed model. The tone of these early fiddles must have been small, owing to the low tension of the gut strings.

In those days, a gypsy orchestra may have been composed of several 'fiddles'; a reed instrument, somewhat like a clarinet, and perhaps one or two psalteries, played with the fingers. This word comes from the old Greek name for a harp, *psalterion*. Later, this instrument may have developed into the dulcimer, which is played with little sticks, and which in its modern form as the cimbalom, is such a feature of Hungarian and Romanian gypsy bands today. The dulcimer or

small cimbalom is supported round the player's shoulders with a strap, or it can be played resting upon his knees. It is believed that the instrument originated in Persia.

There are many songs about the gypsy's love for his violin; here is one of them.

> My father I have never known,
> My mother's long since gone;
> My sweetheart under the flowers lies,
> Of friends I have not one.
> Only you, my violin,
> Are my only friend in the world.

The violin, despite the songs and legends about it, is not the only instrument loved by the gypsies. The Spanish Gitano is inseparable from his guitar, while the Romanian gypsies have borrowed the cobza (a nine-stringed lute) and the nai (the pipes of Pan) besides the cimbalom and piano-accordion.

There have been many famous gypsy musicians whose names have lived on, and whose tunes are still played today. Among these must be mentioned the girl violinist, Czinka Panna, and János Bihári, who was greatly admired by Franz Liszt, when they met in Hungary.

In 1847, when Liszt was on his European tour, he came to Jassy, the capital of Moldavia in Romania, and there, in the drawing rooms of the Boyars, he met the famous Barbu Lautaru (Barbu the Musician). Barbu was an old gypsy with a long white beard, a brilliant violinist, and on that occasion led a small band which played Romanian folksongs to the distinguished company.

Liszt sat down at the piano, saying to Barbu, 'I have heard your music with great pleasure; now, pray, listen to mine.'

Barbu Lautaru
plays to Liszt

The famous pianist began with a prelude, which led into an improvisation of a Hungarian march. . . . Liszt played on and on; never had his performance risen to such heights. When he finished, the applause was terrific. Turning to Barbu, Liszt asked, his eyes shining, 'Tell me Barbu, how did you like that melody?'

The old lautar answered, 'It was so beautiful, Master, that, if I may, I should like to try it myself.'

Liszt's face bore an incredulous smile as he sat by his piano to listen.

Barbu, turning to his little band, put his violin to his neck, and began a Hungarian march. Nothing Liszt had played was forgotten, not a trill, not an arpeggio; all the details of the variations were faithfully followed.

The audience sat entranced, amazement and wonder written on their countenances. When the piece came to an end, Liszt jumped up, and seized two glasses, rushed over to Barbu and exclaimed,

'Drink, Barbu, my master, drink! God has made you a true artist. Indeed, you are a far greater artist than I!'

The following description of the life of a gypsy band leader in Hungary today is taken from the *New Hungarian Quarterly*, No. 30, 1968, and provides an interesting contrast with the note about Barbu.

'The primás (pronounced preemarsh) is a tall well-built man, and his thinning shiny black hair is brushed back. The most gypsy-like thing about him is his eyes, which are brown as walnuts, moist and shiny. He is the leader, and wears a black dinner-jacket. The other musicians wear cherry-red jackets which they hire. Our primás has worked from the age of thirteen; his father was a primás too, and all his ancestors

Famous gypsy violinists of the past: Grigoras Dinicu

were musicians. He can trace his ancestry back to the early
1700s.

The father is the boy's first music teacher. The child is
given several instruments to play with, and the father gets to
know which one the boy is likely to take to. The violin *is* the
gypsy instrument, and all the family want the boy to be a
primás—that's the top of the ladder with the best money.
Socially, too, the primás is held in high esteem. Nowadays,
all gypsy boys take lessons at music schools, and when they
are eighteen, they are examined by a Committee of the
National Light Music Centre. Those who pass, get a certi-
ficate. Some boys grow out of gypsy music and get the desire
to join a symphony orchestra.

There are no illiterate musicians these days—they can all
read music. The ideal gypsy band has eight members—two
primás, second violin, viola, cello, double bass, clarinet and
cimbalom.

Famous gypsy violinists
of the past:
Iancu Iancovici

The primás said, 'When I stand in front of the band, I can tell at once what my public is like. Music affects the audience and the audience affects the music; the atmosphere around midnight is completely different from that of 9 p.m. I never let my players drink, although the customers keep sending them up to us. We mustn't drink—many of us are drivers now. Customers can never ask for a song I don't know—I carry thousands of songs around in my head. If they ask for a local tune I've never heard of, I ask them to hum it once—at the second try I've got it, and the band follows. Improvisation is in our blood.'

This primás speaks several languages, and his Hungarian is precise and clear. He likes classical music, has a record player at home, and all the great violin concertos.

Does he resent the name 'gypsy'? Hungarian Radio ten years ago asked all the musicians how they would like to be called—a folk-orchestra, or a gypsy band, as formerly. They objected to the word 'folk-musicians', but the name was kept officially.

'We are gypsies and our bands are gypsy bands! We don't resent it—we are proud of the name, even if some people use it in a patronising way. We have equal rights before the law, but we know only too well that most people don't like to mix with us in private.'

Hungarian gypsies are snobs too; they do not mix with less important families, and they don't mix with families who are not musicians.

The primás went on, 'We are proud of our family names—Bihári, Dankó, Jancsi Rigó, Lajos Baross, Béla Berkes, Sándor Lakatos, Kálmán Oláh, Imre Magyári.'

The primás was asked, what is the position of women in gypsy families? He replied, 'We don't let our wives and daughters become musicians. Not that they lack the talent, but it's hard work, and not for them.' One couple, the Horváths, play together in a Budapest café.

How many people in Hungary today make a living from music? According to statistics, there are 1,050 restaurants with music in the country, and half of them employ gypsy musicians—that's about 2,000 musicians. How long can a primás keep working? The answer to this was, as long as the bow doesn't drop from his hand.

There is an old primás, Jószef Parádi, who works as a 'standing primás' all through the night, twice a week. He is eighty-five.

The primás ended by remarking, 'Working half the night takes a lot out of you—I don't get to bed before 3 a.m., and you can't lie in—there are too many rehearsals and recordings in the morning.'

61

There are several gypsy legends about the supernatural origin of the violin; the following is one example.

In a dense forest, there lived a beautiful young girl with her father, mother and four brothers. She was madly in love with a handsome gaujo, but in spite of her great beauty, the boy would not look at her. She could not think what to do to attract him, so she called on the Devil to help her.

He was willing to help, but he made certain conditions. 'Give me your mother and father and your four brothers,' said the Devil, 'and your wish will come true.'

From the father, he made a sound box; from the mother, a bow, and from the brothers, the four strings. The six souls had become a fiddle and bow.

The Devil taught the wicked girl how to play it, and her music fascinated the poor gaujo youth who became completely under her spell. One day, she was playing to him on a woodland path when the Devil suddenly appeared between them.

He was angry and discontented with the bargain he had made. 'What!' he exclaimed. 'All that clever magic just for an old man and woman and four striplings? It's not enough—I must have both of you, too!' And with that, he carried them off, leaving the violin and bow on the ground.

Soon, a poor gypsy came along and found the two strange objects; he picked up the fiddle, drew the bow across the strings, and set off for the nearest village. Ever since then, gypsies everywhere have been able to draw tears and laughter by means of the violin.

~4~
Language, Law and Customs

WE HAVE SEEN how scholars and researchers have traced the language of the Romany back to India, and in the book we have used a few gypsy words. We know that the gypsy language is called Romani or Romanes, and that this word comes from rom—'man'.

According to many writers, the purest form of Romany as it is spoken in Great Britain is to be found in Wales.

Charles Duff says that some members of the Wood clan still speak 'deep' Romanes, that is, the almost pure variety spoken by the original Romanies when they arrived in Britain. Romanes as spoken today in our islands is no longer a pure language; it has been debased and almost brought to the level of a complicated slang or jargon.

The original grammar has been forgotten and the modern gypsies use (among themselves) a mixture of English and Romanes, the *pogado tchib*, as they call it, the broken language. Here are a few examples:

Chiv tuti's vast adrey the rai's putsi!
Mandi jin'd what tuti pen'd!

Put your hand into the gentleman's pocket!
I know what you said!

Miro dadrus jalled to buty adrey a wongar mine and his
    pals del'd dado oprey the nok and poggered it.
Father went to work in a coal mine, and his pals hit father
    on the nose and broke it.

Can you roka Romany, can you play the bosh,
Can you jal adrey the steripen, can you chin a kosh?
Can you speak Romany, can you play the fiddle,
Can you eat the prison bread, can you cut a stick?

and lastly,

He kair'd a lot of vongar akai—he's chopped his vardo
for another—mandi dik'd it to-rarti.
He made a lot of money here—he's changed his caravan for
another—I saw it this evening.

Romanes, even the pure variety classified in the family of
Indian languages, includes a vast non-Indian vocabulary.
As it is a language of nomads, it is little wonder that so many
words were dredged from the countries the gypsies crossed or
decided to remain in. Greek, Persian, Armenian, Romanian,
Serbian, Hungarian words are to be found in plenty, but
here is a brief list which demonstrates the similarity between
many Hindi and Romany words.

English	Gypsy	Hindi
aunt	beebi	beebee
luck	bokh	bhagye
great	bauro	bura
ocean	bauri-pani	bura-pani
the sun	can	khan

64

English	Gypsy	Hindi
to kiss	choom	chumb
thief	chor	chor
poor	choro	shori
knife	churi	churi
uncle	koko	caucau
far	dur	dur
black	kaulo	kala
salt	lon	lon
to beg	mang	mangna
woman	manushni	manushi
mouth	mui	mu
fish	mutchee	muchee
foot	peero	parow
old	puro	pura
silver	rup	rupee
gold	sunakai	suna
one	yek	ek
two	dui	du
three	trin	tin
four	stor	tschar
five	pansh	pansch

An interesting sidelight touching on the gypsies' Indian origins was told to me by a Bulgarian journalist. Recently, some Indian films were shown in the capital, Sofia, and the gypsies flocked to the cinemas to see them. While the ordinary Bulgarian patrons had to be content with the sub-titles, the gypsies, it appears, could understand a great deal of the spoken dialogue.

Although a great number of words in basic Romany exist, the large variety of dialects makes confusion for the scholars.

Jean-Paul Clébert, in his comprehensive book *The Gypsies*, says it is difficult even to estimate their number. The principal ones are Armenian gypsy, Finnish, Hungarian, German, Welsh, the dialects of the British gypsies, and the Catalan and Andalusian.

The Spanish Gitanos, as Clébert remarks, have evolved a dialect for themselves—the Caló, which contains not one word from the German.

On the other hand, over 2,000 words from the Arabic are to be found in it. This confirms the passage of the Gitanos to Spain by way of North Africa.

A few words of gypsy origin have found their way into British slang—kosh for stick; pal for brother; moosh for man; munging for cadging, and conk for nose (the gypsy 'knoc' spelt backwards).

Gypsies always seem to be well-informed about what there is to know regarding their clan or tribe, whether it be news about a new baby, the death of an old uncle, where the other part of the family is camping, and what luck they've had, or who has been taken up by the law.

They have no writing, but they possess a very full list of secret signs and marks. This secret code is called the 'patrin', and consists of the use of natural objects and material such as feathers, branches or twigs, pieces of cloth, fragments of marked wood, and even food scraps displayed in such a way that they would not even be noticed by a non-gypsy.

Other signs and marks are chalked or scratched on farm gates or dwelling houses; these inform the next gypsy caller what to expect from the gaujo farmer or housewife.

The method works in the following way. A gypsy woman will call carrying a basket of pegs and a baby wrapped up in

A family sorts out a knotty problem

a bundle. After selling some pegs, the gypsy gets the farmer's
wife into conversation, and learns all about her family affairs
—how many children she has, if there has been illness in the
family, what the husband's likes and dislikes are, whether he
is a heavy drinker or teetotal. As she leaves, she will make
certain unnoticeable marks on the wall or fence.

In a week or two, another gypsy woman will call, and offer
to tell the housewife's fortune maybe. Great will be the good
woman's amazement when she hears intimate details about
her family from a perfect stranger; she will be all the more
likely to believe in the gypsy's dukering, and quite willing to
cross her palm with a little silver.

What do the secret marks look like? They consist in the
main of simple circles and crosses, or combinations of both.
For example, the + or × signs mean 'they give nothing

here', while a circle symbolises 'there is something to be had at this house'.

By means of the patrin, much information can be silently conveyed between gypsy and gypsy; it is really their only way of keeping in touch with each other. Patrin signs used for directional purposes usually consist of bunches of grass laid down by the wayside, twigs laid in the form of a cross (pointing in the direction the family have travelled); bits of rag hung in the bushes, or perhaps just an innocent arrangement of old tins near the ashes of the fire.

Regarding the signs of the patrin, the reader will have to be content with the hints given above; the Romanies will not betray their secrets to the gaujé.

Gypsy law is not contained in gypsy books, for they have no system of writing. It is handed on from father to son by word of mouth. One of the most important of these laws relates to marriage; it forbids marriage between gypsy and non-gypsy, and in the past, the breaking of this law meant banishment from the tribe. Charles Duff's estimate of the number of posh-rats and didakais bears witness to the fact that this old law has been abandoned to a great extent, at least in Britain. According to the law, if a gaujo marries a gypsy girl, he cannot consider himself to have become a gypsy. If he has been on close terms with her family, he might be allowed the title of 'phral'—brother, but he will not be admitted to the secret conferences of the family, and his gypsy bride will be held in contempt by them.

On the other hand, if a gypsy marries a gentile woman, he has the best of the bargain—little disgrace falls upon him, but his new wife must follow gypsy tradition and obey the tribal laws.

The gypsy 'blood marriage' has often been portrayed in films and tales of gypsy life, where the young bride and groom have their wrists cut and their blood intermingled while the gypsy Chief or 'King' performs an elaborate ceremony, the fiddles meantime playing their hearts out. It is uncertain whether this is genuine or a pantomime put on for the benefit of non-gypsy people.

Today, the majority of British Romanies get married in a church or register office, but doubtless they perform some private ceremony of their own in addition.

The reader may have heard the phrase 'jumping the broomstick' as applied to gypsy marriage; but Vesey-Fitzgerald is of the opinion that although a broomstick or branch of flowering broom is sometimes used, it is a tinker custom and not a

Romany one. The form of marriage most frequently practised among British and European gypsies is the simple
joining of hands in the presence of witnesses from both gypsy
families.

Some Romanies include the drinking of pure water from
the same cup, the vessel afterwards being smashed.

As is to be expected with such an ancient race, their customs
contain many 'taboos' or bans, and most of these are concerned with death, food and women. In our days, when television, heart transplants and moon landings are commonplace
occurrences, these taboos make strange reading.

Just as the Jews hold certain animals and fish, like the pig
and the skate, to be unclean, so do the gypsies consider cats
and dogs, even though they keep them as pets.

On the other hand, the horse is usually considered a clean
animal, and not 'mokardi', the gypsy word for unclean in the
taboo sense. Many of these taboos are quite incomprehensible;
while continental gypsies will eat carrion, or the flesh of
animals or birds that have died, they will never knowingly
eat the flesh of a horse.

No gypsy man will eat food a woman has stepped over, he
will throw it to the dogs; and when the men are seated round
the fire, a woman will never pass in front of them. She will
make a detour round the back.

It is general gypsy practice, too, that a woman must not
give birth to a child in a living-waggon; a special tent is set
apart for her, for she is considered mokardi; she even has a
special set of eating utensils for her use during the period of
her confinement. Sometimes, the tent is burned after the child
is born, and the woman returns to live in the waggon once
again.

*Gypsy mother
in Bucharest*

Women's clothing is considered to be particularly mokardi. I once saw an instance of this in London. A gypsy woman selling pegs called at a house and begged for some food; it was not food she really wanted but money. The housewife had just baked an enormous amount of cakes, and believing the gypsy to be hungry, she went inside, filled her apron (which was spotless) with little cakes, and brought them to the door where the gypsy was waiting. On seeing the cakes in the apron, the gypsy's face assumed an expression of horror and repulsion, and she turned away and walked up the path, muttering.

The housewife was astounded at what she thought was ill-mannered ingratitude, and to this day wonders why the gypsy acted as she did.

Women's clothes must not be washed together with those of the men, neither must they be hung up to dry together, and on no account must female clothing come into contact with food.

Today, many of these strange taboos have lost their strength, just as obedience to the marriage laws has become lax. The gypsy man who ôbserves these ancient taboos is not laughed at for being superstitious, far from it, he is respected for keeping the spirit of gypsydom alive.

In romantic novels about gypsies, the novelists often conjured up, for our entertainment, gypsy Kings and Queens holding sway over their subjects deep in the leafy forest. A romantic picture indeed, but Clébert dismisses the idea of Romany royalty as pure journalistic invention, and tells us there never has been a King of the gypsies. It may be that the gypsies themselves have encouraged such tales for the benefit of the gaujé, hoping to gain something from them.

They do however, have tribal chiefs, who are elected, and 'reign' during their lifetime—the honour is seldom passed from father to son.

Also of great importance in the tribe, clan or family is the *phuri dai*—the old woman. She is always a person of great common sense, with long experience and wide knowledge of gypsy laws and traditions. She gives advice on any problem that is likely to arise, and her decision is accepted as final if the chief or head-man is absent.

The gypsies have their own form of justice; it is called the 'kriss', and no real gypsy having a grievance against another would dream of calling in the police or applying to a court of law.

The word kriss has two meanings—the law, and the assembly of elder men who administer it. As with the gaujé, gypsies have their differences of opinion, their disputes about ownership; they too, need to have somebody to give an unbiased judgement about an injury inflicted by a neighbour.

The kriss is entirely the affair of the men; women can appear only as witnesses, but the phuri dai can be asked for her opinion. In the past, the death penalty was included in the list of punishments which could be inflicted on a guilty person. In a gypsy court of law, a man of great experience, called the 'krisnitori', presides over the assembly, seated on a carpet-covered chair or stool; the council of elders squats on the ground. To some, these words may conjure up an amusing picture, but the proceedings are far from funny for the man in the dock. For his crime against the law or another member of the tribe, he can be banished, be given severe corporal punishment or suffer mutilation.

If the accused is found to be not guilty, a celebration will be held, and the acquitted man will spill some of his drink to appease the spirits. From all accounts, gypsy trials are scrupulously fair, and it is the krisnitori who is prosecutor, judge and executioner of the sentence. Obviously, the krisnitori must be a fair-minded, well-balanced man with wide knowledge of gypsy tradition and law.

73

A Hungarian dance, about 1665 (from an old print)

The Romanies are not devoid of religious beliefs, but as regards a definite religion as understood by the gaujé, they have none; if it is useful or convenient for them, they will accept one (or more) of the religious faiths flourishing in the country of their adoption.

The gypsy has always made the best of things, and in the past, when Mohammedan Turks occupied a country in which they were, they cheerfully decided to switch from Christianity to Islam.

The Romanies are not atheists—far from it; they have a God, who is called 'o Del' or 'o Develo', meaning *the* God. Satan is called 'o Beng'. In Christian countries, the Romanies seem to be more attracted by the Roman Catholic or the Greek Orthodox faiths than by the Protestant; this may be solely due to the colourful pomp and ceremonial and the beautiful interiors of the churches, especially in South-eastern Europe where the prominent religion is Greek Orthodox.

Gypsy belief is crammed with legends and mythology, and the following story is a sample of one of them. It was told to me in a mountain village in Transylvania, and its subject is the Creation.

'O Del, wanting something to do, decided to try and make a man. He took some lime, spit, and a little salt, made a figure, then laid it in his bread oven to bake. It was such a lovely day that he went for a walk to the top of the mountain, and quite forgot the little figure cooking in his oven. He hurried back, opened it, and there the little man was—burnt quite black.

'This was the first Negro. Sighing, o Del made another figure, put it in the oven; this time, he was so afraid of burning it that he opened the oven too soon. The image lay in the dish, pale as chalk, so he made this one the ancestor of the white folk. "Perhaps I'll do it right this time," o Del said, so he made a third figure and carefully timed the cooking.

'Success at last! The little man was done to a turn, a rich chestnutty copper brown. And this was the first gypsy.'

According to some observers, the Romanies could be said to be nature-worshippers. Martin Block has seen them removing their hats to the moon, and surely the sun, the life-giver, receives more than a little attention from them. The Kalderash tribe are said to address a prayer to each new moon when it appears, asking for luck, good health, and much money. This custom, however, is not an exclusive gypsy one; many people in Britain say, 'Look, a new moon! Make a wish, and turn your money over!'

Fire, earth, water and wind all have special meanings for gypsies, but it is only with great difficulty that they can be encouraged to speak about these things.

The gypsies have no use for repentance for sins committed in the Christian sense—the only sin they understand is violation of their gypsy laws. Theft or lying are not sins to them, and as they do not usually lie to or steal from each other, they do not feel in need of forgiveness.

To the gaujé, one of the most spectacular things about a Romany funeral is the burning of the deceased's caravan. Newspapermen come from miles around to view the spectacle, and, it must be admitted, it makes good copy. Block tells us that among certain tribes in Germany this custom is discontinued, and the vardo is sold, just as it is, to non-gypsies.

I have a feeling that in Britain today, the actual waggon in which the owner lived is no longer burned, but a smaller cart or an old lorry that once belonged to him is sacrificed to the flames. The custom, which is of great antiquity, is really a sacrifice to the dead.

As the gypsy is born under the open sky, so must he die. At the point of death, he is carried out from his vardo or tent, and made as comfortable as possible on some blankets, and of course, with an awning to keep off the rain or blinding sunlight. The dying person makes no complaint—he is content to abide by the law.

In countries such as Britain, where births and deaths must be registered, a church burial complete with parson is conducted for the deceased; according to the gypsies, the priest or parson is endowed with magical powers, and these powers are highly valued by the relatives. At all events, the dead man must have a 'good funeral' with plenty of wailing and tears; they believe that he will appreciate a highly emotional demonstration. Abroad, if the gypsy was a famous primás, a gypsy band will accompany the coffin to the cemetery.

A few years ago when Maria Tănase, a famous and much loved gypsy singer, died in Bucharest, the whole city came to a standstill, and Romanies from the remotest parts of Romania came and played at her funeral. A great funeral with musical honours took place fairly recently in Budapest, when the death occurred of a famous primás.

In some parts of Europe, the corpse is taken to the grave with the coffin uncovered; I have seen this on at least two occasions in rural Romania, but the custom is frowned upon by most people today.

Personal belongings the dead man valued are placed in the coffin with him—his violin, his medals or pipe or some other favourite object, and most important of all, a coin for him to pay his fare across the river to the land of the dead. At the graveside, a relative will pour some wine on to the coffin and on the earth when it has been filled in.

From that day, the dead man's name must not be uttered again, for the dead are taboo, and the gypsy is fearful of 'mulos' or ghosts.

Almost everywhere, bereaved gypsies fast until after the funeral, taking only bread and water, but the children are not expected to do so, and are given food.

Gypsies' coffins are made unusually large, and this is because the corpse is often buried fully clothed; suits and overcoats, or in the case with women, several dresses and domestic articles, are placed in the coffin. Instances have been recorded both here and abroad when the body was dressed in clothes turned inside out. Why? For luck, perhaps? How often has a parent been heard to exclaim, 'Oh, that's lucky—don't change it!' when one has put on a sock or jumper inside out?

~5~
Tents, Caravans and Dress

IT IS AGREED by scholars that the gypsies, when they first left India, had no horses, mules, donkeys or oxen, and that they started their great trek to the West on foot, carrying their belongings on their backs. Nobody can be sure of this, for there are no records. Nobody seems to know, either, just when the gypsies adopted the typical 'gypsy caravan', the colourful living waggons used by travelling showmen; before this, they used carts and light waggons with canvas or felt hoods.

The genuine gypsy is a tent-dweller; he loves living in the open air, and feels stifled and imprisoned in four walls.

Some of the house-dwellers and half-settled gypsies put up a tent in the garden and live in it during the summer. Every kind of shelter from a simple interlacing of branches with a carpet or blanket laid over it, to a proper tent with a frame of curved rods and covered with good canvas can be a gypsy's home.

According to Martin Block, who made a great study of gypsy ways, the shape of the tent varies. Three kinds exist, one with a high pointed top, one unpointed and low, and a third semi-circular. Any sort of material can be used to cover the frames—canvas, rush matting, bark, old blankets or

79

water-proof ground-sheets. According to Clébert, the tent is called 'tsaro' and sometimes 'khera'. It is interesting to compare this word with another Mongolian word for a tent, which is 'gher'—could this be another link with Central Asia?

The Rudari in Transylvania, the makers of baskets and spoons, build for themselves semi-underground dwellings, with a roof of branches and earth. Inside the single little room is a fireplace, and a pipe to carry the smoke away sticks up out of the earth. The bed is made of wooden planks a foot or so off the earth, covered with reeds or a rush mat. Pieces of wood and cloth serve as wall-covering, and a cauldron hangs from a chain. These are very snug dwellings.

When the Rudari decide to move on, they destroy the little homes, later to build new ones where a good supply of timber is to be had for their work.

The gitanos of Granada, Godella and Valencia live in caves, and are a regular attraction for tourists. These caves, and others in Spain, have been inhabited for hundreds of years, ever since the troubled times when Jew, gypsy and Spaniard found refuge from the Moorish invaders. Today, the caves are kept clean and attractive, and the gitanos extract good sums from the camera-happy tourists by their performances of graceful Spanish dances to the sound of guitars.

'Gypsy caravans' are a well-known feature of Romany life; they are called *vardo* in Romanes. Although designs vary considerably, there are five main types of living waggon—the bow or barrel-topped, the Ledge, the Reading, the open lot, and the showman's. Regrettably, the horse-drawn vans are disappearing from our roads, and the modern Romany has taken to motorised living vans, with built-in furniture, radio and television sets and Elsan-type closets.

The barrel-topped van is also called a Leeds, because the type used to be built near that city; the Reading waggon, too, was named after the town of Reading and because the builder of this type had his premises there. The vardo called the Ledge is the one most likely to be seen; all the leading van builders turned out this type of wagon. In describing vardo, the differences between them can be shown far easier in pictures than in words.

The vardo is a complete one-roomed dwelling on wheels,

Barrel-topped waggon

with sleeping accommodation, heating and cooking appliances, with lots of space for crockery, linen and clothing, domestic articles, and food. To enter, you mount the detachable steps at the front, which are between the shafts. There are windows at the back and sides, and some models have a skylight.

At the back of the van there is a rack or 'cratch', and underneath a large cupboard or 'pan-box' in which is stored food and kitchen-ware.

As you enter the vardo, the stove is on the left-hand side, and its chimney-pipe, double-sheathed to prevent scorching, sticks out through the roof. The sleeping place is at the far end of the van, and is usually in the form of a double bunk.

Opposite the stove, there is a locker, which serves as a storage place and seat. The stove is used mainly for warmth and comfort; cooking is usually done in the open, and in the summer, the owners prefer to sleep in the open too, regardless of the comfortable feather beds awaiting them inside.

Highly polished brass-work, figured mirrors and carved woodwork make the best type of vardo an attractive home. You would find many mantelpieces decorated with quite valuable china figures, and the 'best' china-ware (cups, saucers and plates) are usually of very good quality.

It is quite rare for gypsies to build their own vardo, partly because they lack the skill, and they would begrudge the time needed to be spent on the job; to build a first-class vardo would take a carpenter and wainwright about six months.

The timber used is oak for the main frames, red deal for the ribs, top and flooring, ash for the wheels, and polished mahogany for interior fittings. From eight to ten coats of

'Open Lot' vardo

83

paint, plus several of varnish, ensures that the exterior can resist the hot sun, and the rains and snows of winter.

Favourite colours used for vardo painting are post-office red, crimson, deep yellows, warm blues and greens; on the van door and on the pan-box horses and other animals, birds, fruit and flowers are painted. The horse is a favourite subject, and if the gypsy cannot find anyone to paint one, he will use a transfer.

Skylight waggon

There are still several skilled vardo decorators in the country, who specialise in original designs, painting scrolls, flowers, horses' heads, freehand and without copying. Black as a colour is unpopular among Romanies, as they believe it to be unlucky, but it is sometimes used for outlining a scroll or bunch of fruit. Similar design work is sometimes to be seen on canal barges, and it really comes under the title of 'folk-art'.

There are several taboos and superstitions affecting the gypsy's vardo. When a Romany takes possession of a new vardo from the builder, he will at once break one of the windows 'for luck'. It is a serious matter for him if, by chance, a member of his family has died, or a child has been born in it; the van is then considered 'mokardi', and must be either sold to a gaujo, or destroyed by fire.

To avoid such a hazard, gypsies take care to see that births and deaths take place in a tent set apart.

What is the gypsy's national dress? The answer is he has none; men and women dress in the style of their adopted country. They do not spin, or weave cloth as do the peasants, and are content to buy new, second hand, or to beg cast-off clothes from the gaujé. In the warmer countries, the children go about quite naked until they are about ten or eleven years old. The adults dress in anything that comes to hand. The British gypsies and their children cannot be said (in the majority of cases) to be poorly dressed—and some of their younger women are quite fashionable.

It is important to remember that no Romany would ever dream of wearing the clothes of a gypsy who had died, but he would have no objection to the clothes from a dead gaujo. In many countries (and no doubt in Britain) the second-hand clothes shops do a fair amount of business with gypsies. In warmer climates, the gypsy does not seem to care what tattered rags he wears; he goes on wearing them until they fall to pieces.

In Hungary they are fond of wearing high boots, and the musicians in the cafés are sometimes to be seen sporting unusual military uniforms in vivid colours adorned with silver coins. Until recently, the Romanian gypsies went about bare-footed; nowadays they have taken to wearing boots and shoes, but these they are glad to kick off when back in camp.

Where the Spanish gitano has the look of a Spaniard, the English Romany wears a trilby hat or cap, and usually in the impudent gypsy way. They are fond of coloured kerchiefs (dikló) worn round the neck, the favourite colours being red or yellow.

Romany women everywhere wear their pleated skirts long, and it may be asked—what happens when a woman needs a replacement? It is certain that she will not make one for herself; she will find a gaujo dressmaker and order one or several to be made, if she cannot buy it off the peg.

Both men and women are extremely fond of jewellery and trinkets, and wear gold and silver ear-rings, bracelets and necklaces made from old coins from nearly every Western European country. Even in Britain, gypsies are to be seen wearing small gold ear-rings.

With regard to other kinds of adornment, tattooing is popular among some Balkan and Western Asian types. It is done only on the face, and it serves as a means of defence against evil spirits; only one colour is used, blue, and the designs, which are always geometrical ones, all have special meanings.

Eating, Medicine, Washing and Water

THE GYPSY will eat almost anything, except what he considers taboo. These items being discounted, he has a wide choice of eatables from everything that moves or grows.

Much of the poultry and game that goes into the pot is obtained by poaching, and the gypsies do not look upon this act as theft. Their view of the matter is that the fruits of the earth belong to God and to all men.

The Romany is very skilled in the art of poaching, and it is said that British gypsies invented the artificial fly for trout and salmon fishing. They make a fishing bait which is impregnated with gum from a certain aromatic plant, and which never fails to attract the fish. The properties of this plant have been known for centuries in Western Asia.

When good solid food is in short supply, the gypsy will make do without complaining; he worries far less about his calorie intake than the average gaujo, but tobacco he must have. If he cannot obtain it, he will use dried leaves and stalks cut up for his pipe or cigarettes.

Most writers on gypsy subjects maintain that the hedgehog is a favourite gypsy dish, and they describe the several ways of preparing and cooking this creature; this may be so, but I believe that they enjoy beef, pork, mutton, or poultry just as well. They are not particular if the meat is fresh, either—in fact, they have been known to eat fish and meat which by us would be condemned as rotten. And yet they do not seem to suffer many ill-effects.

Gypsies declare that the flesh of an animal that has died naturally tastes better than that of those which have been slaughtered.

When bread is wanted, the gypsy wives buy it locally in the various countries—they hardly ever bake it for themselves.

In South-eastern Europe, where cultivated fields of melons and pumpkins are to be found growing, anyone, including the gypsies, is allowed to help himself to a few for immediate consumption (but not to take them by the load and sell them!).

In the autumn the woods are full of berries, crab-apples and other fruit, and these make a welcome addition to the gypsy larder. The women do not preserve fruit; they prefer to buy dried fruit or jams from the local shops. Neither do they prepare and smoke meat and bacon to make salami. Such items of food are always purchased.

Stews are always popular items on Romany menus; one advantage of them is that the young children can tend a slowly-cooking stew while the adults are away at their work. The Romany is not too concerned about what goes into the pot, or for that matter, where it came from. Should the police come snooping around the camp searching for clues in the shape of feathers or fur, they are not likely to find much evidence upon which to bring a charge!

The favourite drink of the British gypsy is tea; a cup of tea made over an open fire under the trees wants a lot of beating—somehow, it seems to taste far better this way than taken from bone china cups in a drawing-room. Central European gypsies also have the tea habit, but drink it without milk.

Romanies in other parts of Europe take coffee and wine, but when neither is to be had, pure water from a mountain stream will serve to quench a gypsy's thirst. On special occasions like a wedding or a re-union, they can consume an enormous amount of alcohol, but they scarcely ever become drunkards. During family celebrations, the dead are not forgotten; nobody speaks their names, but their memory is silently honoured by the ancient custom of spilling a little of the wine or spirit upon the ground.

Gypsies usually adopt the food and drink habits of the country in which they live, and in Britain, besides tea, the gypsy is fond of his pint at the local, especially when he is attending a fair, whereas in Hungary and Romania he will drink the wine of the country.

Among primitive people, illness has always meant the presence of demons in the body. To effect a cure, the demon had to be driven out. In the seventeenth century the practice of medicine was still based on the teachings of the great founders of the art, Hippocrates and Galen, but it had become discredited by all kinds of ridiculous theories as to the causes of disease.

These theories were not based upon observation or experiment, but were built up by certain people who were seeking a cut-and-dried 'system' covering all diseases, upon which cures could be effected. An unlucky patient's illness had to match up with the 'system' then in fashion, and he had to suffer the treatment of the day—Sweating, Blood-letting, Purging, or Dieting.

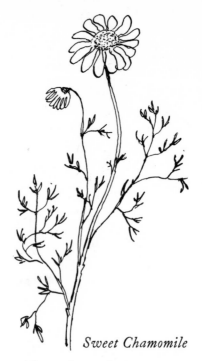

Coltsfoot   *Sweet Chamomile*

Much of gypsy medicine today (though perhaps not so much in Britain) is based on similar antique theories, and to make matters worse, so-called magic is also employed, with the use of putrid matter such as human and animal excrement, urine, bear's grease, dead beetles and frogs' livers.

Although gypsy cures are largely based on herbal remedies, a great deal of superstition and mumbo-jumbo is connected with illness and its treatment. The gypsy seldom calls in a doctor because he has more faith in the remedies of the phuri dai.

As we have said, it is remarkable that the Romanies, in spite of their lack of cleanliness, manage to keep in such good health. They have a great knowledge of herbs, and for centuries have treated themselves from concoctions infused from leaves and berries or ointments for wound dressings.

 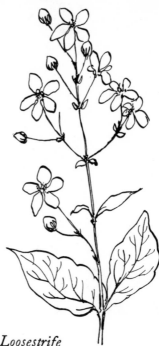

Greater Celandine   *Yellow Loosestrife*

Although the health of the average Romany is fair enough, he, in common with all mankind, suffers from indispositions from time to time. Rheumatism, catarrh, hooping cough, insect bites, worms, corns and warts, bronchitis, biliousness, constipation, diarrhoea, heartburn and so on can be relieved or cured, the gypsies believe, by the use of many of our common wayside plants.

Coltsfoot (*Tussilago farfara*). Asthma and bronchitis can be relieved by smoking the dried leaves, while the juice from fresh ones is made into an ointment for ulcers and sores.
Sweet Chamomile (*Anthemis nobilis*), drunk as tea, cures flatulence or 'wind'.
Celandine (*Chelidonium majus*) is used for warts and corns on the toes.

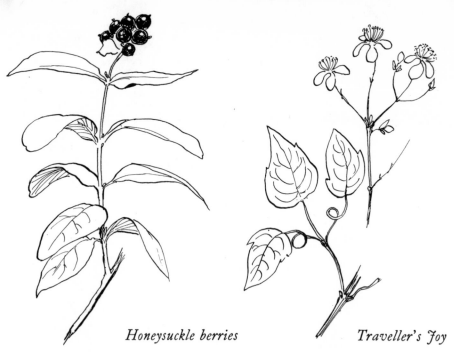

Honeysuckle berries   *Traveller's Joy*

Mouse-ear Chickweed (*Cerastium vulgatum*). The leaves boiled and drunk as tea cure coughs, and so does
Horehound (*Marrubium vulgare*).
Loosestrife 'tea' (*Lysimachia vulgaris*) is good for diarrhoea.
Honeysuckle berries (*Lonicera periclymenum*) relieve a sore throat.
Traveller's Joy (*Clematis vitalba*). Tea made from the leaves is good for rheumatism.
Marsh Mallow (*Althaea officinalis*) heals sore eyes, and relieves insect stings.
Eyebright (*Euphrasia officinalis*), drunk as tea, cures coughs. When used as a lotion it heals sore eyes. (Gypsy children often suffer from sore eyes, caused by flies.)
Solomon's Seal (*Polygonatum multiflorum*). If a gypsy party ends up in a fight, an ointment made from the leaves of this plant and applied to a bruised eye will remove the dis-

Marsh Mallow   *Solomon's Seal*

coloration.

There are a great number of plants used in gypsy medicine, in fact, a whole book could be devoted to their preparation. Many of the substances dispensed by chemists originate from quite common plants which grow here and abroad. The gypsy word for these medicinal plants is 'drab'.

Effective as the herbal remedies are, the phuri dai will sometimes resort to 'magic' for her cures, such as catching a black slug and transfixing it on a thorn bush as a cure for warts, the idea being that as the slug dies, the wart will shrivel and fall off!

Amulets and talismans are worn by Romanies in a little bag around the neck, and such bags may contain a spider, or a piece of frog-skin to keep away rheumatism, or be filled with a 'magical' selection of roots, little pebbles and a dried snail.

With the exception, perhaps, of the younger generation of gypsies, the Romany hates water. Only very seldom will he wash, and it is a never-to-be-forgotten day when he takes a bath. His grubby skin is always coated with a layer of body-grease; among many of the gypsies in the rural parts of Eastern Europe, soap is quite unknown.

It is said that they use some kind of leaf to clean their skins, as do certain tribes of Mongols in Central Asia. It is remarkable how comparatively healthy the gypsy remains, in spite of his dirt and parasites. When we are young, we are exhorted to remember that 'cleanliness is next to godliness', but we don't seem to enjoy much better health than the gypsy! It should be said at once that the living waggons of most English gypsies are cleaner than many a gaujo home, but this happy state does not always apply to gypsies in other parts.

The Romany not only has an aversion to washing in water, he hates travelling on it as well. When an unfortunate gypsy is sent to prison, the first thing he has to undergo is a bath and a haircut; I have read accounts about gypsies in Hungary and Romania who, being forced to bath and have their heads shaved for hygienic reasons, burst into such a torrent of wailing and lamentation that one would think they were about to be executed.

This fear and dislike of washing is very deep-seated in the Romany race. It is perhaps one of the main characteristics of a nomadic civilisation, where the inhabitants of the steppe and arid desert have first to give the precious water to their animals, only afterwards quenching their own thirsts and keeping a little by for cooking purposes. In these circumstances, to waste water for washing clothes or themselves is considered a crime.

We who live in snug houses with good, always drinkable

piped water, can have no idea what real thirst can mean. We take water for granted, not realising that to people who live in dry areas, that simple commodity can sometimes mean the difference between life and death. Among the nomadic peoples of Central Asia, a child is washed at birth, thereafter he seldom takes another wash throughout his life.

In Genghis Khan's code of laws, the Yassak, it was a crime to bathe or to wash clothing in running water during a thunderstorm; Clébert writes that to break this law meant a sentence of death. Other historians assert that the Mongols used to wear their clothes until they fell to pieces. When one is confronted by a troupe of ragged, dirty, parasite-ridden gypsies, one is led to conclude that there is an ethnic link between the gypsies and the Asiatic Mongols of old.

Another point is that the Mongols, generally speaking, cannot swim, and when forced to take a journey in a boat, become giddy and seasick. Moving water has the same effect on the gypsy when he has to make a journey by ship.

As we have seen, the evidence of the linkage of their language with Sanskrit provides a tidied-up answer to the tantalising question of where the gypsy came from. This is a very attractive hypothesis. Yet could it be that the gypsies are a far older race of people than we have hitherto supposed, and that they did *not* originate in India, but came from Central Asia to that country, say, about 1,500 years ago?

There is another thing, a small thing it is true, but there is the basic similarity between the yurta of the steppe-dwelling nomad and the 'bender tent' used by the gypsy.

The strong flavouring of Hindi words in Romanes may indicate that they spent a very long time indeed in India, before pushing on to the West. Could it be, then, that their aversion to wasting water for hygienic purposes is an instinct brought down with them from their Central Asiatic days? The gypsy has his own set of values for 'dirty', 'clean' and 'unclean' (mokardi). He does not mind being filthy and unwashed himself (that's clean dirt—if you wash, you wash off your luck) and yet he will throw his plate of dinner away if one of his womenfolk should happen to step across it.

7

The Gypsy in Modern Society

IT IS NOW TIME for us to consider the question of how the gypsies fare in the world of today. For centuries they have been, and still are, as much a part of the population as the farm worker in his cottage, the lord in his manor, the coloured immigrant or the refugee. Very many of them served in the two World Wars in defence of their country have fought and died or lost their limbs with the rest of us.

In spite of this, are our Romanies treated as equal citizens? For all our traditions of 'fair play for the under-dog', it is sad to relate that they are, on the whole, treated very badly in Britain, and our efforts to deal with the gypsy problem (if a problem exists) lags behind those of many other European countries. I write the words 'if a problem exists' deliberately. The word 'problem' means 'a matter difficult of settlement or solution'; the gypsies' requirements are quite modest—all they want is to be allowed to continue their nomadic way of life, not to be eternally chivvied around by hostile local authorities, and the provision of proper camping sites, with a hard standing, water, and toilet facilities.

And that is all. Gypsies are very independent people, and

97

can always make a living at their traditional crafts.

It is interesting to look at the 'problem' posed by the gypsies in modern society and compare what is done for them in the various countries in which they live.

In dealing with the gypsies, the first aim of any government in charge of this 'floating population' is to discourage their nomadism. This causes, and will always cause, deep resentment among the Romanies because nomadism is the only life they know. However, they are responding to the efforts made in some countries to give them a settled way of life.

Greece

For the gypsies, life in Greece today is rather more pleasant than it is in the British Isles. Three ways of living are open to them; the first is the nomadic one of travelling about the country in the manner of their ancestors; the second way is for them to live on a piece of land allotted by the State, take a regular job, and send the children to school where free elementary and higher education is open to them. If the children do well, there is nothing to prevent them attending a University. This naturally brings with it opportunities for higher paid posts.

Gypsies who choose the third way of existence in Greece live in villages where they may form over 90% of the population. The 1951 census gave the number of Greek gypsies as 7,400.

The Netherlands

In the Netherlands, the Dutch government has provided about 300 permanent camping sites, with water and toilet facilities. Small school buildings have been erected close to the 'camps' for the benefit of the children; the number of Romanies in Holland is small in comparison with other countries.

Germany

There are over 30,000 gypsies living in the German Federal Republic, and here they enjoy considerate and sympathetic treatment. They are allowed to travel about the country if they wish, and good camping grounds are at their disposal. Strangely, the children are not compelled by law to attend school, and only about a quarter of them do so. The adults are encouraged, but not forced, to give up their nomadic habits, and to take regular work and live in settled homes.

Sweden

In Sweden, the gypsy population is small, there being only 800 to 1,000; the State has made strenuous efforts to educate them, helped them to find settled homes, or aided them to purchase living waggons. The government exerts no pressure—if having become settled, a family wishes to take to the road again, it is free to do so.

In 1958, the government tried to solve the gypsy question by giving them steady settled jobs, and it was hoped that with regular incomes, the gypsies would buy or rent houses and send their children to school. The scheme was not successful, because the male gypsies were quite untrained for regular employment, and could not even read or write. Nevertheless, the task of housing them was taken in hand, and by 1965, 96% of the families were living in houses or flats. A family can have a State loan to buy furniture, and education is quite free for children, as well as adults.

It is reported that school attendance is irregular, and most of the men still prefer their own gypsy occupations to regular work in industry.

Finland

Over 4,000 Romanies live in Finland. They first came there from Sweden in 1559; they enjoy full citizenship, all gypsy children must attend school, and the young men have to do military service. More than half the Romanies live in houses, but during the summer months, some take to the road again. A branch of a government ministry looks after gypsy affairs, and one of the members of the committee is a gypsy.

Czechoslovakia

In Czechoslovakia, the problem is different. With a population of 200,000 gypsies and travellers, the State has opened engineering and other craft schools, where the young men become useful workers; those among them who happen to be musicians earn extra money playing at weddings and other festivities.

Despite attempts by the government to prevent nomadism, it is thought that only about 10% lead a settled life. An aid scheme exists for gypsies wishing to settle, through which they can buy a house, repaying the loan over 30 years.

Belgium

There are very few gypsies in Belgium, perhaps only a hundred or so. Conditions for them are not pleasant, and they are driven from pillar to post by fussy local laws, as they are in many parts of Britain. No heed is paid to the problem of education for the youngsters, and there is certainly no provision of proper camp sites as in Sweden.

France

Conditions are uncomfortable also in France, which has about 80,000 gypsies and travellers. An old law of 1912 compels the French 'Bohemians' to carry an identity card which must be shown to the police on entering or leaving a district. The French regard the gypsies as unwelcome vagabonds, and limit their stay in a place to forty-eight hours. Because of this, no gypsy children can attend school in a regular way, unless the family settles down to a gaujo life. Clébert lists the details the identity book must contain; not only the names, the country of origin, date and place of birth of the bearer are required, but also the height, colour of eyes, chest measurement, breadth of head, length of right ear, length of fingers, length of left foot, and length from left middle finger to elbow! Furthermore, two photographs and finger-prints must be included.

Fortunately, there are many kind-hearted people in France who are working for the betterment of the poorer gypsies, and to have the degrading identity card abolished, or at least, many of the obnoxious requirements contained in it.

America

As regards gypsies in America, it has not been possible to discover how they are treated there; one must assume that they have to conform to the laws of the State in which they find themselves. From reports, they keep to their traditional trades—work with various metals, musicians, fortune-tellers, dancers, pedlars, etc, and they make more use of the motor car, the telephone, supermarkets; some of them use cheque-books to pay their accounts.

Bulgaria

In Bulgaria, efforts have been made by the State to prevent nomadism. Education for the children is compulsory, and a great number of families live in little houses, while one-fifth of the gypsy population, including many of the women, have

regular jobs. Bulgaria has a large number of gypsies, and they all have full citizen rights.

Many of them earn their livings as entertainers and showmen; other groups find employment in engineering, building and in general industry.

Hungary

Hungary's large gypsy population of 250,000 all have full citizenship. As with other Eastern European governments, the Hungarians have tried their hardest in getting the gypsies off the roads, or out of the dreadful hovels in which they lived before the Second World War.

Many of the Hungarian Romanies have become educated, have fixed addresses and permanent employment; among them can be found highly skilled workers, teachers, and even doctors. Over 80% of all gypsy children now go to school; epidemics that once took a sad toll are now almost eliminated, and fewer gypsy babies die, thanks to the Hungarian government's vigorous measures.

Of course, there are still thousands of Romanies who want no part of this new civilisation, and who are still content to travel the country, playing their music, or undertaking odd metal-working jobs.

Italy

According to the 1963 census of Romanies in Italy, about 9,500 live in that country. We have no up-to-date report of their treatment there, but it is known that they are engaged in scrap metal dealing, horse-coping, metal, wood and basket work, and naturally, music and entertainment. We note also that about 5% are doing agricultural work, which is rather unusual.

USSR

In the great land mass which comprises the Soviet Union, the government's practical measures for settlement and steady employment of Russia's 132,000 Romanies have been only partly effective. Nevertheless, they are treated with consideration, and some of the larger Russian towns provide schooling for children and adults, using Romanes as well as Russian. It is encouraging to note that the Russians are anxious to preserve the rich folklore and customs of the gypsies.

Poland

Poland's 30,000 gypsies are encouraged to settle down by the offer of permanent jobs plus the benefits of a free health service, education, and the provision of houses and flats. But always the policy of compulsory settlement is resented by the free-living Romanies, and many of them have been reported as travelling west through Austria, preferring to take the 'pot luck' offered by the open road.

Romania

Enquiries as to the gypsies' lot in Romania elicit the reply that 'there is no gypsy problem here'. All of Romania's 105,000 gypsies have equal rights, in fact, according to the socialist ideals prevailing in that country, the very word gypsy or 'tigane' is thought to be insulting to them.

Settlement is encouraged but is not compulsory; a free health service, education and opportunities for regular work is offered to them, and many have taken advantage of it, especially the musicians and metal-workers. The gypsies I met throughout the country no longer have that typical servile look; usually their faces are open and frank, and they all seem happy and contented. It is a far cry from the days when they were slaves of the Boyars, with no human rights whatever—when they were starved, and beaten to death if they tried to escape.

In Transylvania I came across a gypsy colony who were living near a new engineering plant. When the factory began to operate, the gypsies were offered regular jobs in it. At first, only a few accepted, because they said 'it was difficult for them to give up their free life', but the guaranteed wages, improved living conditions—most of them were offered flats in newly-built apartment houses—have convinced even the most stubborn advocates of nomad life to change over to a new way of living.

I met one of the Romanies, a woman of about twenty-five years of age, in her elegant flat in Aiud. Her husband was now a lorry driver, and she invited me to come in and wait until he returned.

'Come in and sit down and listen to some music—we have over fifty records of folkmusic. Excuse me being busy—I have to change the bed-linen and get a meal for the children coming home from school!' What a change for the better in the lives of this Romany family! They were not forced to settle, they chose it of their own free will.

I met many other Romanies in Bucharest, pure-blooded gypsy men, coming from a long line of musician ancestors. Most of them played in the State Folk-orchestras, lived in blocks of flats in the capital, and earned a good living; all, without exception, were perfectly content and happy with their lot.

Other musicians I met live on the outskirts of the city, and are content to be lazy and dirty, taking the occasional job playing at weddings or funerals; these people are different material from the settled musicians, and are called 'mahala' people by the ordinary citizen. The word means 'low life', gutter or slum dweller; it can also mean 'the outskirts or suburbs'.

As I have written, Romanian gypsies are not compelled to settle, and in support of this, I have seen strings of barrel-shaped vardo drawn by skinny horses in the remote country-side. The men's faces were of the darkest brown, making quite a contrast with the paler gypsy musicians who live in the city.

Spain

The gypsies, or rather the gitanos, seem to enjoy the greatest freedom in Spain, and one which the gypsies of Britain may well envy. They are at liberty to wander and to work at their traditional trades.

Britain

In Britain, Romanies need the goodwill of the non-gypsy population, town and rural councils and so on, if they are to live their lives in peace.

We have a special problem in that we are living in a densely populated country; every square inch of land belongs to someone, or to a local council, and with a few exceptions nobody wants gypsies on their doorstep. The gypsy will not easily tolerate being tied to one spot, and yet if he is to be accepted by modern civilised society, he must support himself as well as paying a proportion of the money it costs to keep up the roads he travels on, the water he drinks, and everything else to which a price is attached in this modern, highly-organised world.

Since the powerful crusade on behalf of the British gypsies begun by the late Norman Dodds, M.P., the public has become aware of their plight, and of the ruthless persecution practised against them by heartless district councils and landowners. Mr Dodds, who became Member of Parliament for Dartford, Kent, in 1945, began his fight after visiting a large gypsy camp on the Belvedere Marshes. 1,600 people lived on this site (only a third of them being real gypsies), and for most of the year the place was a sea of mud, amongst which children played and hordes of hungry dogs searched for food.

For readers who would like to delve deeper into recent gypsy history, I recommend them to Mr Dodds' book

One reason for mistrust of the gypsies

Gypsies, Didikois and Other Travellers (Johnson Publications 1966); they may care to take up the torch on behalf of our Romanies, who are handicapped because they usually cannot read or write, and cannot use clever words.

In 1951 Mr Dodds formed and organised the Gypsy Committee and produced the famous Gypsy Charter. His valiant fight, which had wide newspaper, radio and TV coverage, and which brought the plight of the gypsies to the notice of the British public, has greatly eased the lot of the Romanies. In 1966 the Gypsy Council was formed; this is an established organisation linked to groups in other countries. And now, the voice of the Romany counts for something at last in Britain. At least, there is hope.

Let us for a moment briefly examine the feelings of the gypsies and their reaction to the average rate-paying house-dweller. Romanies have great difficulty in dealing with officials because they do not know the law and cannot read or write. They cannot understand the attitude of the officials who, having made them move on, know quite well that there is nowhere they can legally camp in the next district.

Everywhere the Romany sees his traditional 'hatchin-tans' (stopping places) being closed to him, and views this as an attack by officialdom to stop him earning a living. Because of constant harassment, the Romany views most gaujé with deep suspicion; this makes him evasive and shifty, and seldom can a true answer be obtained from him.

He feels he is despised as an inferior person; he is aware of the fact that very few employers would give him a chance; many publicans refuse to serve him (they put notices up in the bar which read 'No gypsies served here'); he knows that his children are singled out at school as 'dirty gypsies'.

In return, he has only contempt for officials and house-dwellers. There has been no sign on the part of the public to wish to see the gypsies' lot improved, to see their children educated or to give them proper camping sites, let alone to elevate them from the position of despised outcasts.

Ratepayers often object strongly when schemes for the benefit of gypsies are proposed. Why, they ask, should any-thing be done for these low people? Why don't they simply give up their uncomfortable life, move into a house, and live like proper human beings?

As we have seen in these pages, notwithstanding the hard-ships of just managing to live and keep healthy, and the hostility of officials and non-gypsies, the Romany persists with his way of life which has the deep-rooted traditions of over a thousand years.

This ancient race of people are not just 'drop-outs', failures rejected from normal society, but an ethnic group living in the past, which has been overtaken by today's circumstances. In some ways, the gypsy life is a poor, sad life, but there are many compensations in the form of warm family unity, the freedom which comes from being their own masters, of being able to eat and sleep under the stars and yet remain healthy.

After a lifetime of living in the open air, free as the wind, free to shout and laugh or quarrel, to suddenly take to living within four walls would amount to a complete revolution for the Romany. It would mean that new habits, together with behaviour and conduct becoming to a member of civilised society would all have to be learnt.

I wonder how a house-dweller would get on if he was forced to give up his comfortable home and secure job, take to a vardo and the open road (with few legal stopping places) and feed and keep his family in good health by doing some job in which the arts of reading and writing were quite unnecessary?

Not long before this book went to press, the first World Romany Congress to be held since 1935 took place at a school in the Kentish countryside. Representatives of more than 3,000,000 gypsies in Eastern and Western Europe, India and America arrived at Heathrow Airport to spend a few days at Cannock School, near Orpington, where they discussed international problems.

In their neat suits, they looked more like business-men than members of the gypsy race, and carried brief-cases instead of the usual tattered violin case. Only one member, Janko Jovanovici, had an instrument with him, a balalaika.

Mr Gratton Puxon, general secretary of Britain's Gypsy Council, addressed the delegates; although not a Romany himself, he speaks Romanes, and is a pillar of strength for the gypsy cause in Great Britain. He expressed the hope that an

A Bender tent

international congress can be held every two years.

What did the Congress achieve? The delegates exchanged news and views about conditions in their own particular countries, but it is difficult to see what solid work can be achieved in improving the life of British and foreign gypsies except through, perhaps, the United Nations Organisation.

On the Easter Bank Holiday after the Congress, a Gypsy Festival was held on London's Hampstead Heath. Londoners had the opportunity to see and hear many foreign gypsy singers and musicians. The show was well organised, and the large audience saw the blue and green gypsy flag hoisted—blue for the sky and spiritual values, green for the land with its symbolism of Earth.

Some musicians from Czechoslovakia performed, as well as Janko Jovanovici with his balalaika; guitarist Jean Fernandez, a gitano from the North of France; Raya, a female singer from Yugoslavia; Maissa Rouda, a fiery dancer and singer, Russian-born; Fred Wood, a British gypsy, sang poaching ballads and cracked Romany jokes; last and not least, a Hungarian group of three musicians thrilled the audience with traditional Hungarian and Romanian folk-songs, played on violin, cimbalom and double-bass.

Between the musical items, a gypsy 'bender' tent was erected; these are composed of cut sticks bent over to form a rough dome, with the ends stuck into the ground. Old blankets and rags were thrown over it to form a tent. Many poor wanderers have been born in such make-shift tents, which even today afford a rough night's shelter for the traveller.

After some speeches, some paraffin was poured over the tent, and it was ceremoniously burned in memory of the gypsies who fought and died in the Second World War.

The Festival closed with the procession of St Sarah, the patron saint of the gypsies. She represents the Christian form of the Indian goddess Kali, and according to a gypsy who was present, 'She has been respected by the Romanies since they left their original homeland in Northern India a thousand years ago.'

Musicians followed the statue of the saint, and coloured streamers, pegs and flowers were thrown over it for luck.

In conclusion, it is to be hoped that our British Romanies can now look forward to a new era of confidence where persecution and harassment have no place. Practical steps have been taken by enlightened ministers and members of the government, and lately we are happily becoming aware of new permanent camping sites being opened, with everything a gypsy wants—a hard standing for his vardo or lorry, water and washrooms, and education for his children.

Interested readers may like to know that there is a society devoted to gypsies and their affairs. It is called The Gypsy Lore Society and it was formed in 1888; its object is to enlarge the study and knowledge of the Romanies wherever they may be; to study their language and dialects; to investigate gypsy problems which may arise, and to publish information in the Society's Journal with the view of enlarging the public's interest; this may have the effect of gaining their sympathy for and understanding of the Romanies.

Letters should be addressed to

Miss Dora Yates, Litt.D., M.A.
Honorary Secretary,
Gypsy Lore Society,
The University Library, LIVERPOOL

Bibliography

The author gratefully acknowledges the help obtained in the preparation of this book by the study of many of the following volumes; titles, authors and publishers will serve as a guide to further reading on British and foreign gypsies.

Books

Alder, M.   *My Life with the Gypsies* (Souvenir Press 1960)

Bercovici, K.   *The Story of the Gypsies* (Cape 1928)

Block, M.   *Gypsies* (Methuen 1938)

Borrow, G.   *Gypsies of Spain* (Murray 1907)

Clébert, J.-P.   *The Gypsies* (Vista 1963)

Dodds, N.   *Gypsies, Didikois and Other Travellers* (Johnson 1966)

Duff, C.   *A Mysterious People* (Hamish Hamilton 1965)

Hall, Rev. G.   *The Gypsies' Parson* (Sampson Low)

Levy, J.   *As Gypsies Wander* (Faber 1953)

Starkie, W.   *Raggle-Taggle* (Murray 1929)

Vesey-FitzGerald, B.   *The Gypsies of Britain* (David and Charles)

Webb, G.   *Gypsies: The Secret People* (London 1960)

Yoors, J.   *The Gypsies* (Allen and Unwin 1967)

Papers and periodicals

Figuri de Lautari (Bucharest 1960)
Gypsies and Other Travellers (HMSO 1967)
The Journals of the Gypsy Lore Society
New Hungarian Quarterly (Budapest 1969)
New Hungary (Hungarian News and Information, London)
The Romanian Folklore Institute (Foreign Languages Publishing, Bucharest 1959)

Index

117

Romany, 8, 63; *see* Gypsy
Russia, 14, 15, 29, 52, 103, 111

St Sarah, 111
Saxony, 14
Scandinavia, 26
schools, 27, 28, 29, 98, 99, 100, 101, 102, 103, 104, 105; *see* education
Scotland, 15, 32
sea travel, 14, 95
Serbia, 14, 64
shoe-blacks, 43
sign-language, 31, *see* patrin
silver, 36
singing, 35, 36, 77, 110
Sinti, 32, 49
slaves, 29
Sofia, 65
Spain, 14, 15, 28, 32, 57, 66, 80, 86, 106
stopping-places, *see* hatchin-tans *and* camping sites
Sweden, 15, 26, 100
Switzerland, 14
Syria, 14

taboo, *see* mokardi
talisman, 93
Tanase, Maria, 77
tarot, 47
Tartars, 23, 44
tattooing, 86
tents, 79ff, 80, 85, 95
tinkers, 19, 33, 35, 69
tin-plating, 36, 40
tobacco, 87
trades, *see* occupations

Transylvania, 14, 32, 75, 80, 104
tribes, 31ff, 72
Turkey, 15, 32

unclean, *see* mokardi
university, 98
Urban, Reinhold, 20
USSR, *see* Russia

Vali, Etienne, 11
vardo (caravan or waggon), 70, 76, 79ff, 94, 105, 109, 112
verbunkos, 54
Vesey-Fitzgerald, 69
Vienna Gazette, 10, 11
violin, 52, 53, 54, 55, 57, 58, 59, 62, 77, 111
voivodes, 29, 30

waggon, *see* vardo
Wales, 14, 18, 32, 63, 66
washing, 94, 95, 96, 112
water, 94, 95
whitewashing, 33, 35, 39, 40
women, clothing, 16, 54, 71, 72, 85, 86; taboos, 70–3, 96
Wood, 63; Fred, 111
woodcarving, 13, 33, 36, 42, 103; bowls, 35; sieves, 40; spoons, 35, 37, 80
World Romany Congress, 109–111
world wars, 97, 111
writing, 66, 69

Yassak, 95